S0-AWF-735

COLLECTOR'S GUIDE TO

TOOTSIETOYS®

SECOND EDITION

Identification & Values

DAVID E. RICHTER

COLLECTOR BOOKS

A Division of Schroeder Publishing Co., Inc.

The current values in this book should be used only as a guide. They are not intended to set prices, which vary from one section of the country to another. Auction prices as well as dealer prices vary greatly and are affected by condition as well as demand. Neither the Author nor the Publisher assumes responsibility for any losses that might be incurred as a result of consulting this guide.

Cover photo designed and constructed by David E. Richter.
Photographs by David E. Richter

Tootsietoy® is a registered trademark of the Strombecker Corporation.

Should you have any comments on the information in this book or have Tootsietoy items available for sale, you may write to David Richter, 6817 Sutherland Ct., Mentor, OH 44060

Searching For A Publisher?

We are always looking for knowledgeable people considered to be experts within their fields. If you feel that there is a real need for a book on your collectible subject and have a large comprehensive collection, contact Collector Books.

Cover Design: Sherry Kraus
Book Design: Benjamin R. Faust

Additional copies of this book may be ordered from

COLLECTOR BOOKS
P.O. Box 3009
Paducah, Kentucky 42002-3009

@$19.95. Add $2.00 for postage and handling.

Copyright: David E. Richter, 1996

This book or any part thereof may not be reproduced without the written consent of the Author and Publisher.

Printed by IMAGE GRAPHICS, INC., Paducah, Kentucky

CONTENTS

ACKNOWLEDGMENTS

Special thanks first to my wife, Jean, for her support, understanding, and helpfulness once again with my second edition of *Collector's Guide to Tootsietoys*. She helped with some of the proofreading and made many good suggestions to make this book a success.

I would like to thank my brother, Danny, for the good times we had at the toy shows we attended through the years. He helped remove my Tootsietoys from their wall cases to be photographed and later put them back in their rightful places.

Once again I relied on my sister-in-law, Gerri, to proofread for me, correct all the minor errors I made in spelling, etc. Anything I asked her to do, she said no problem I can do that. Thanks again, Gerri, for your hard work and support.

Many thanks to all the antique dealers and toy dealers I corresponded with either in writing or in person at various shows. I would like to thank all my many collector friends for either supplying a group of photos to use in my book or answering some of my many questions. They are not in any special order, Steve Butler, Gates Willard, William Hartley, and Richard Langfellow for keeping an eye out for the seventies toys which I desperately needed to complete my new chapter on seventies Tootsietoys.

I purchased many of the seventies toys pictured in my book from Richard Langfellow. Hans Stang for the use of his Cannon camera and several nice pieces from his collection I did not have in my own collection to photograph. A special thank you to my good friends Steve and Anna Marie Oznowich for their support and also for supplying me with many pieces from their collection of Tootsietoys. Also for the great times we've had since we met, whether attending shows together or just going out to dinner for an evening.

A special thank you goes to Myron B. Shure, chairman of the Strombecker Corporation, for his permission to do this new book and use the product name TOOTSIETOY, and for supplying me with many copies of the 1970s catalogs giving me the much needed information and dates I need for my research.

Finally, thanks to William Schroeder of Collector Books. The editor of Collector Books, Lisa Stroup, for her support in making this book a success. If I missed anyone, it wasn't intentional. Thanks to all the book dealers who carried and sold my value guide, and all those who wrote to me with information, and supported me with my project.

David E. Richter

INTRODUCTION

To toy collectors, antique dealers, and car buffs everywhere:

I would like to welcome you to my second edition of *Collector's Guide to Tootsietoys*. This new edition combines the 1970s toys with earlier pre-war and later post-war toys. Prices were averaged between some auction results on Tootsietoys, actual selling prices at shows, and dealers price lists I received in the mail. Tootsietoys are starting to become extinct at flea markets and antique shows. These were good sources in the past to obtain new items for your collection. I myself rely on the larger toy shows to hunt and search for the pieces I still need to complete my vast collection of Tootsietoys. Just when you think you have seen all the variations a new one pops up out of the blue. A good example would be the 3" 1949 Ford Pickup with a solid closed rear window. It is pictured in the Truck and Semis chapter.

The first Tootsietoy toys were produced around 1910 by a company called Dowst. Tootsietoys are still being produced today under the Strombecker Corporation name, a division of Tootsietoys. The newer type toys of today are half metal and half plastic with soft black plastic tires.

Single toys in their original packaging and boxed sets of Tootsietoys of all years are much sought after by everyone. The prices realized at some toy shows and auctions make me wonder if prices will ever level out. It does not seem to be the case with Tootsietoys and other collectible items.

My wife, Jean, also likes to attend the many types of shows with me. She is searching for that kewpie doll she doesn't have or perhaps a bargain on a basket for her collection. I myself just enjoy getting out and meeting new people, and if I'm lucky will find a toy for my collection. At any rate the fun is in the search and in trying to pluck out that bargain item from a large show.

I hope you will enjoy reading and looking through my value guide whether you are a longtime dealer or a brand new collector to this terrific hobby of collecting Tootsietoys.

I wanted to include the huge assortment of dollhouse furniture but I had no replies to my ads for information and photographs of the many neat detailed pieces.

I welcome your comments and letters about Tootsietoys. After 30 years of collecting I am still learning new information about America's first and oldest toy company.

HISTORY

Strombecker is the oldest toy company in the United States, dating back to 1876. The Dowst Brothers Company was started to publish the *National Laundry Journal*. They made the collar button and several different laundry accessories.

Samuel Dowst in 1893 saw a new type-casting machine located at the World's Columbian Exposition. He recognized the possibility of making molds to cast the collar button from lead or similar type metal. The start of the die-cast industry was born thanks to his success with making molds for the collar button. This small but great achievement was the early beginning of the die-cast industry.

The evolution toward Tootsietoy products continued to prosper rapidly. Many miniatures were made for various industries — miniature flat iron, shoe, skillet, plus many more. These trinkets were gathered together and sold to the candy industry as prize items to be put in their penny packages. This great effort by Dowst was the start of a strong toy die-cast process.

The year 1914 saw the first successful toy production: Henry Ford's very famous Model T. Around 50 million attractively packaged Tootsietoy Model T's were produced. Tootsietoy is a name that has continued today to dominate the die-cast toy industry with its many attractive packaged toys and their excellent realism.

The Tootsietoy name applied to only some of their die-cast products. It wasn't until after a Dowst brother had a granddaughter named Toots, they decided to name the doll furniture toys after her. The trade liked the name so well it was adopted for all of the company's die-cast toys.

The Cosmo Manufacturing Company was established by Nathan Shure in 1892, to make small novelties for Cracker Jack and other candy firms — a similar business to the Dowst Brothers Company. In 1926, the two die-cast giants merged together calling their new company, Dowst Manufacturing Company. They produced many replicas of the various GM models, Fords, and other popular cars on the road at that time. Tootsietoy was seeing a great need to appeal to the youngsters and besides its realistic brightly painted cars, decided to add doll furniture, train sets, farm sets, and airplanes of that era to its line.

The children who played with Tootsietoy products not only grew up, but passed their enthusiasm to not only their children, but their children's children.

The large demand for all the various Tootsietoy products grew so rapidly that a new modern plant was constructed to meet the demand for their attractive and varied items.

In 1961, Shure's descendants purchased Strombeck-Becker, makers of electrically-powered plastic cars. Henceforth, the company adopted the Strombecker name and is still called Strombecker Corporation today.

Toy collecting today is a very popular hobby, enjoyed by many serious collectors of all age groups. Tootsietoy vehicles are among the most sought after and are quite valuable to collectors today. Quite a number of Tootsietoys that were once bought for five and ten cents are now between $50.00 and $100.00 and up.

I personally think Tootsietoy products are not only great toys for children and collectors now, but will be preserved and passed on for generations to come.

HOW TO USE THIS GUIDE

Chevrolet Panel Trucks, 3"

Beside or under each photograph within this guide you will find the following information: the catalog number of the Tootsietoy shown, the name of the toy, the year the toy was made, and the years it appeared in various catalogs. An example is 1950 – 1960. Prices are given for toys in each of the following three conditions:

The first truck on the left is an example of a toy with about 90% of its original paint. This toy is fine having only small paint chips and all its tires on its axles.

The middle truck is an example of a toy with about 95% of its original paint and only slight wear on the tires and high points of the toy's body.

The last truck on the right is an example of a toy with 100% of its paint. This toy should have no tiny imperfections or chips. These toys in mint state will bring you a better return for your money down the road.

TOOTSIETOY VALUE GUIDE

90% — Fine, having only small paint chips and at least 90% of the original paint on the body.

95% — Slight wear on tires and the high points on the body. This toy should have at least 95% of the original paint on the body.

100% — No imperfections or chips and having 100% of paint. The last price being brand new or in an absolutely mint state.

Please note that almost all of the Tootsietoys from 1970 – 1979 have several decals or stickers on them. Please take into consideration the condition of decals and stickers when purchasing a piece for your collection. If possible, upgrade your set or collection when a mint piece comes along. Like other collectibles, the best condition will bring a high price in the future when reselling your items or toys.

AIRCRAFT AND SPACESHIPS

The first Tootsietoy plane No. 4482 Bleroit was issued around 1910. The earlier version of the small 67mm plane had small spoked wheels — later models had the solid disc type wheels. The tiny No. 4650 with its match-like crossed struts to support the wings was issued in 1926. The small yellow and red plane is quite scarce today and is probably well underrated in price. It was only produced just a few years in the 1920s.

The No. 119 Army plane of 1936 is one of the most common pre-war era planes. It came in assorted colors and later around 1939 – 1941 was even camouflaged. Camouflaged planes of all types are quite scarce today and sure would be a welcome piece to anyone's collection.

Tootsietoy No. 722 the DC-4 Super Mainliner not pictured in my last book, finally appears as not only a silver civilian liner, but as an Army Transport and the really scarce Tootsietoy DC-4 camouflaged Bomber. The Transport and Bomber were camouflaged in tan and green, and also light blue with tan. The latter is more rare.

The Navion and the F-94 Starfire, for the most part, are the most common postwar planes. They are available at all your local toy shows and flea markets.

I would say almost all of the various types of airplanes pictured in this chapter were placed in boxed sets with other airplanes or with accessories such as small three-piece baggage carts, loading ramps, tiny die-cast pilots, and badges of various airlines with their names on them.

No. 4482
Bleriot Plane, 1910
$80.00/$100.00/$120.00

No. 4650
Biplane, 1926
$95.00/$110.00/$125.00

No. 4660
Aero-dawn, 1928
(early wheel type)
$55.00/$70.00/$85.00

No. 4660
Aero-dawn, 1934
$50.00/$65.00/$80.00

No. 106
Low Wing
1932
$60.00/$75.00/$90.00

No. 107
High Wing
1932
$60.00/$75.00/$90.00

No. 04649
Ford Tri-motor
1932
$95.00/$110.00/$125.00

No. 4675
Bi-wing plane
$45.00/$60.00/$75.00

No. 4675
Bi-wing Seaplane
$50.00/$60.00/$75.00

No. 4660
Seaplane
$55.00/$70.00/$85.00

No. 4659
Autogyro, 1934
(early wheel type)
$80.00/$95.00/$120.00

No. 4659
Autogyro, 1934
$75.00/$90.00/$115.00

No. 720
Fly-n-Gyro
1938
No Price Available

No. II9
U.S. Army plane
1936
$45.00/$60.00/$75.00

No. II9
(camouflaged)
$50.00/$65.00/$80.00

No. 717
DC-2 TWA, 1937
$60.00/$75.00/$90.00

No. 718
Waco Bomber
1937
$95.00/$110.00/$125.00

No. 718
Waco Dive Bomber
1937
$105.00/$125.00/$140.00

No. 719
Crusader
1937
$70.00/$85.00/$100.00

No. 125
Lockheed Electra
1937
$45.00/$60.00/$75.00

No. 717
DC-2 TWA
1942 – 1946
$65.00/$80.00/$95.00

No. 1030 Dirigible
(Los Angeles), 1937
$70.00/$85.00/$100.00

Buck Rogers
(Flash Blast Attack Ship)
1937
$95.00/$110.00/$125.00

Buck Rogers
(Battlecruiser)
1937
$95.00/$110.00/$125.00

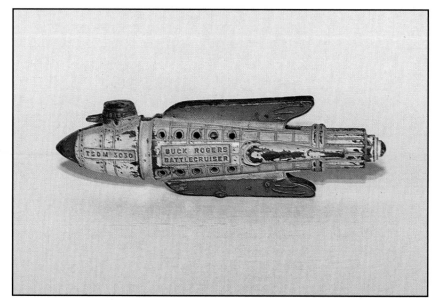

Buck Rogers
(Venus Duo-Destroyer)
1937
$95.00/$110.00/$125.00

No. 721
Curtis P-40
1941
$150.00/$175.00/$200.00
NOTE: Prop not three bladed.
Should be.

P-80
Shooting Star
1948
$20.00/$25.00/$30.00

Piper Cub
1948 – 1952
$15.00/$20.00/$25.00

Navion
1948 – 1953
$15.00/$20.00/$25.00

Beechcraft Bonanza
(cast prop pin)
1948
$30.00/$35.00/$40.00

Army Bonanza
(note: decals)
1948
$30.00/$35.00/$40.00

Beechcraft Bonanza
1950
$15.00/$20.00/$25.00

Twin Engine Convair
1950
$75.00/$85.00/$95.00

Coast Guard Seaplane
1950
$100.00/$130.00/$150.00

F-86 Sabre Jet
(2 piece body)
1950
$15.00/$20.00/$25.00

F-86 Sabre Jet
(1 piece body)
1956
$10.00/$15.00/$20.00

Panther Jet
(2 piece body)
1953 – 1955
$20.00/$30.00/$40.00

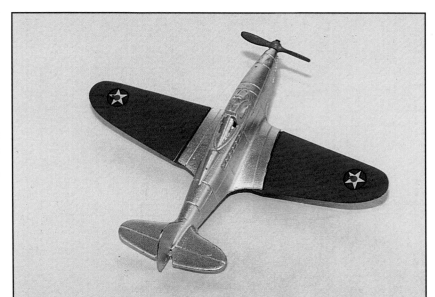

P-39 Fighter
1947
$100.00/$130.00/$150.00

P-38 Fighter
1950
$80.00/$95.00/$105.00

Lockheed
Constellation
1951
$90.00/$120.00/$135.00

Boeing
Stratocruiser
1951 – 1954
$80.00/$95.00/$105.00

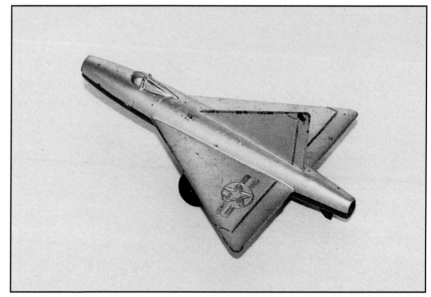

Delta Jet
1954 – 1955
$20.00/$30.00/$40.00

Panther Jet
(1 piece body)
1956 – 1969
$10.00/$15.00/$20.00

F-94 Starfire
1956 – 1969
$10.00/$15.00/$20.00

F-94 Army Jet
1956 – 1969
$15.00/$20.00/$25.00

Navy Cutlass
1956 – 1969
$10.00/$15.00/$20.00

F-40 Skyway
1956 – 1969
$10.00/$15.00/$20.00

F-40 Skyway
(two-tone)
1956 – 1969
$15.00/$20.00/$25.00

Army Cutlass
1958 – 1960
$15.00/$20.00/$25.00

United DC-4
Super Mainliner
1941
$75.00/$85.00/$95.00

"Army" DC-4
Transport
1941
$90.00/$100.00/$110.00

DC-4
Long Range Bomber
1941?
$150.00/$175.00/$200.00

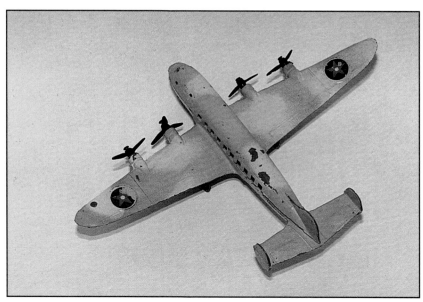

Boeing 707
1958
$35.00/$45.00/$55.00

Hiller
Helicopter
1968 – 1969
$30.00/$35.00/$45.00

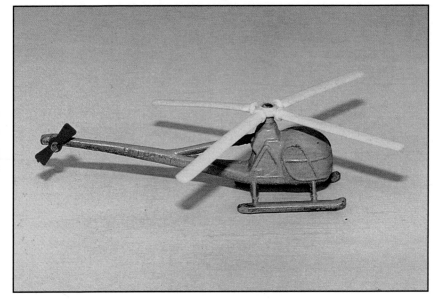

DC-4
Long Range Bomber
(bottom)
$150.00/$175.00/$200.00

Bleriot Plane
The World Flyers Toy
1925
No Price Available

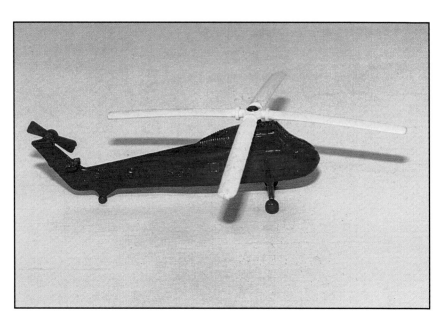

Sikorsky S-58
Helicopter (rare)
1958 – 1969
$40.00/$65.00/$85.00

Barclay plane, with
piggyback Tootsietoy Midget
St. Louis
1936
$35.00/$55.00/$75.00

AUTOMOBILES AND RACERS

The first Tootsietoy auto was the small No. 4528 Limo produced around 1911. It came in black, dark blue, and dark green. Early examples of this model had tiny spoke-type wagon wheels trimmed in gold. In later years, the wheels were all painted black. This toy, like a few other earlier toys, was not marked by the company.

Lincoln Zephyrs, La Salles, and the Graham series cars and vans are really tough to locate for sale — especially in mint condition. The above pre-war toys were nicely detailed with their own shiny metal grills and bumpers along with white rubber tires mounted on their own rims.

The rarest post-war model in the three-inch series would still be the Nash Metropolitan convertible. The rarest four-inch postwar, I think, would be the 1941 Chrysler Windsor convertible. The rarest six-inch series would be the 1950 Chrysler with its delicate windshield still in place.

Since my last book's printing I have managed to upgrade almost 75% of my vast Tootsietoy collection to mint or near mint models. Hope you enjoy this new expanded chapter on Automobiles and Racers. Elsewhere in this book, you will find separate chapters on just the Graham models and the GM series models of the 1920s and 1930s.

No. 4528 Limousine 1911 – 1928, 2" toy.
$30.00/$45.00/$60.00

No. 4570
Ford Tourer
1914 – 1923
$30.00/$40.00/$50.00

No. 4570
Ford Tourer
1924 – 1926
$30.00/$40.00/$50.00

No. 4629
Yellow Cab Sedan
1921 – 1933
$30.00/$35.00/$45.00

No. 4636
Buick Coupe
1924 – 1933
$40.00/$55.00/$70.00

No. 4641
Buick Tourer
1925
$40.00/$50.00/$60.00

No. 4655
Ford Model A Coupe
1928
$35.00/$45.00/$55.00

No. 4666
Large Bluebird Racer
1932 – 1941
$30.00/$45.00/$55.00

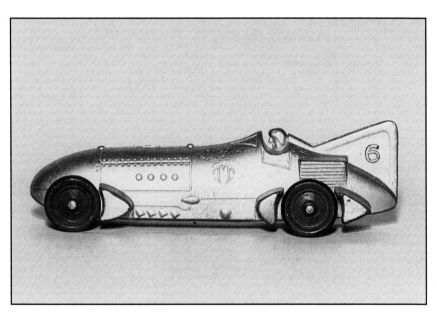

No. 4666
Large Bluebird Racer
1932 – 1941
(disc wheels)
$30.00/$45.00/$55.00

No. 23
Small Racer, 1927
(rare)
$55.00/$80.00/$105.00

No. 6665
Ford Model A Sedan
1928
$40.00/$50.00/$60.00

No. 101, 102, 103, 110
Two-inch models
1932
$25.00/$35.00/$45.00

No. 716
Doodlebug
1935 – 1937
$75.00/$85.00/$95.00

No. 712
La Salle Sedan and Coupe
1935 – 1939
$125.00/$175.00/$245.00
NOTE: The same toy with tan
painted top was the
convertible model.

No. 713
La Salle Sedan
1935 – 1939
$120.00/$170.00/$240.00

No. 6016
Wrecker
1937 – 1938
$200.00/$270.00/$350.00

No. 6015
Lincoln Zephyr
1937 – 1939
$200.00/$270.00/$350.00

1934 Ford Coupe
$50.00/$65.00/$80.00

1934 Ford Convertible Coupe
$60.00/$75.00/$90.00

1934 Ford Sedan
$50.00/$65.00/$80.00

1934 Ford Convertible Sedan
$60.00/$75.00/$90.00

1935 Ford Convertible Coupe
(rare)
$75.00/$100.00/$125.00

1935 Ford Convertible Sedan
(rare)
$75.00/$100.00/$125.00

No. 0111
1935 Ford Sedan
$35.00/$45.00/$65.00

No. 0112
1935 Ford Coupe
$35.00/$45.00/$65.00

No. 0116
1935 Ford Roadster
$40.00/$50.00/$70.00

No. 0118
DeSota Airflow
1935 – 1939
$35.00/$45.00/$60.00

No. 1016
Auburn Roadster, 6"
1936 – 1941
$30.00/$40.00/$55.00

No. 1016
Auburn Roadster, 6"
1942 – 1946
$25.00/$35.00/$50.00

No. 1017
Jumbo Coupe
1936 – 1941
$35.00/$45.00/$65.00

No. 1017
Jumbo Coupe
1942 – 1946
$30.00/$40.00/$60.00

No. 1018
Jumbo Sedan
1936 – 1941
$35.00/$45.00/$65.00

No. 1018
Jumbo Sedan
1942 – 1946
$30.00/$40.00/$60.00

No. 1043
Ford & Trailer
1937 – 1941
$50.00/$70.00/$90.00

1935 Ford Fire Chief Car
1938 – 1940
(sold in sets only)
$125.00/$175.00/$225.00

230 La Salle
Sedan, 3"
1940 – 1941
$25.00/$35.00/$45.00

230 La Salle
Sedan, 3"
1947 – 1952
$20.00/$30.00/$40.00

231 Chevy Coupe
1940 – 1941
$25.00/$35.00/$45.00

231 Chevy Coupe
1947 – 1952
$20.00/$30.00/$40.00

232 Open Touring
1940 – 1941
$35.00/$45.00/$55.00

232 Open Touring
1947 – 1952
$30.00/$40.00/$50.00

233 Boat Tail Roadster
1940 – 1941
$25.00/$30.00/$35.00

233 Boat Tail Roadster
1947 – 1952
$20.00/$25.00/$30.00

239 Station Wagon
1940 – 1941
$30.00/$40.00/$50.00

239 Station Wagon
1940 – 1941
(rare color)
No Price Available

239 Station Wagon
1947 – 1952
$20.00/$30.00/$40.00

Austin-Healy, 1956
6", 1959 – 1964
$25.00/$35.00/$45.00

Buick Station Wagon
1954, 6"
1955 – 1959
$30.00/$35.00/$45.00

Buick Experimental
1954, 6"
1958 – 1964
$40.00/$45.00/$50.00

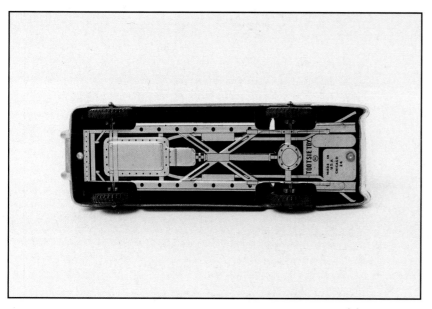

Buick Experimental
Note: Detailed tin bottom (rare)
$40.00/$45.00/$50.00

Buick XP-300
1951, 6"
1953 – 1959
$35.00/$45.00/$60.00

Buick Roadmaster
4-door, 1949, 6"
1949 – 1950
$35.00/$45.00/$55.00

Buick Estate Wagon
1948, 6"
(open grill)
$55.00/$65.00/$75.00

Buick Estate Wagon
1948, 6"
(closed grill)
$60.00/$70.00/$80.00

Buick Roadster
1938, 4"
1947 – 1949
$35.00/$45.00/$55.00

Cadillac 60
4-door, 1948, 6"
1949 – 1954
$25.00/$35.00/$45.00

Cadillac 62
4-door, 1954, 6"
1955 – 1959
$30.00/$40.00/$50.00

Cadillac 62
4-door, 1954, 6"
1955 – 1959
(tow hook model)
$35.00/$45.00/$55.00

Cadillac 62
4-door, 1954, 6"
1955 – 1959
(tin bottom model)
$55.00/$65.00/$75.00

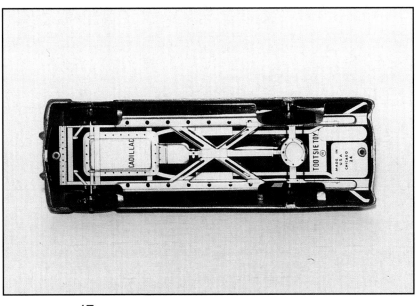

Chevy Fastback Coupe
(white wood wheels)
1942?
$30.00/$40.00/$50.00

Chevy Fastback Coupe
(black tires)
1947 – 1949
$25.00/$35.00/$45.00

Chevy Fastback Coupe
Note: No fender trim
$35.00/$45.00/$55.00

Chevy Bel Air
1955, 3"
1956 – 1958
$15.00/$20.00/$25.00

Chevy Fastback
1950, 3"
1951 – 1954
$15.00/$20.00/$25.00

Chrysler New Yorker
1953, 6"
1953 – 1954
(semi-rare)
$25.00/$35.00/$45.00

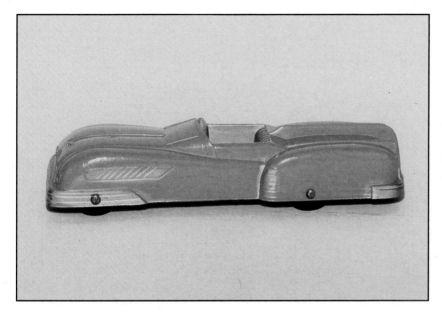

Chrysler Experimental
Roadster, 6"
1947 – 1949
$30.00/$40.00/$50.00

Chrysler Windsor
Convertible, 1941
4", 1947 – 1949
$25.00/$35.00/$45.00

Chrysler Windsor Convertible
1950, 6"
1951 – 1955
$75.00/$95.00/$125.00

Chrysler Convertible
1960, 4"
1961 – 1964
$15.00/$20.00/$25.00

Ferrari Racer
1956, 6"
$25.00/$35.00/$45.00

No. 1046
Station Wagon
1940 – 1941
$45.00/$60.00/$75.00

No. 1046
Station Wagon
1947 – 1949
$35.00/$45.00/$65.00

Corvette Roadster
1954 – 1955
4", 1955 – 1969
$20.00/$30.00/$40.00

Ford B Hotrod, 1931
(1961 issue), 3"
1961 – 1969
$15.00/$20.00/$25.00

Ford Convertible
1949, 3"
1949 – 1954
$20.00/$25.00/$30.00

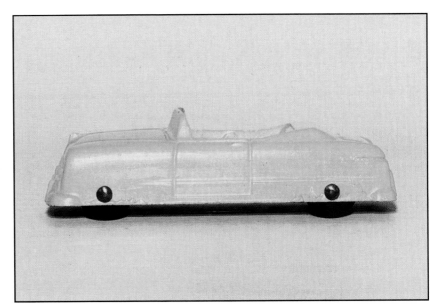

Ford Sedan
4-door, 1949, 3"
1949 – 1954
$20.00/$25.00/$30.00

Ford Mainliner
4-door, 1952, 3"
1953 – 1954
$25.00/$30.00/$40.00

Ford Customline
1955, 3"
1955 – 1958
$20.00/$25.00/$30.00

Ford Fairlane 500
Convertible, 1957
1959 – 1969
$15.00/$20.00/$25.00

Ford Ranch Wagon
1954, 3"
1955 – 1960
$20.00/$25.00/$30.00

Ford Ranch Wagon
1954, 4"
1955 – 1960
$25.00/$30.00/$35.00

Ford Station Wagon
1959, 6"
1959 – 1967
$20.00/$25.00/$30.00

Ford Station Wagon
1960, 3"
1962 – 1964
$15.00/$20.00/$25.00

Ford Station Wagon
1962, 6"
1964 – 1968
$25.00/$35.00/$45.00

Ford Falcon
1960, 3"
1961 – 1964
$15.00/$20.00/$25.00

Ford, 1940, 6"
(1960 issued)
$35.00/$45.00/$50.00

Ford V-8 Hotrod
1960, 6"
(with & without tow hook rear)
$20.00/$25.00/$30.00

Ford LTD, 1969, 4"
1970
$15.00/$20.00/$25.00

Jaguar Type D
1957, 3"
1959 – 1960
$15.00/$20.00/$25.00

Jaguar XK 120
1954, 3"
1955 – 1960
$15.00/$20.00/$25.00

Jaguar XK 140
Coupe, 6"
1959
$20.00/$30.00/$40.00

Kaiser Sedan
1947, 6"
1947 – 1949
$40.00/$50.00/$60.00

Lancia Racer
1956, 6"
$25.00/$35.00/$45.00

Lincoln Capri
2-door, 6"
1953 – 1958
$25.00/$35.00/$45.00

Mercedes 190 SL Coupe
1956, 6"
1959 – 1964
$25.00/$35.00/$45.00

Mercury Custom
4-door, 1949, 4"
1950 – 1952
$25.00/$35.00/$45.00

Mercury Fire Chief Car
1949, 4"
1953 – 1960
$35.00/$45.00/$55.00

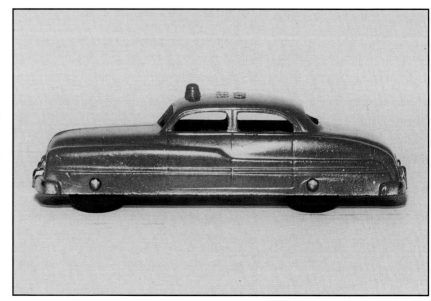

Mercury
4-door, 1952, 4"
1953 – 1954
$20.00/$30.00/$40.00

MG TF Roadster
1954, 3"
1955 – 1960
$20.00/$25.00/$30.00

MG TF Roadster
1954, 6"
1959 – 1967
$25.00/$35.00/$40.00

Nash Metropolitan
1954, 2¼" (rare)
1955 only
$45.00/$55.00/$65.00
NOTE: Two axle variations
in photo.

Offenhauser Racer
1947, 4"
1947 – 1969
(rubber & plastic tires)
$15.00/$20.00/$25.00

Oldsmobile 88 Convertible
1949, 4"
1950 – 1954
$25.00/$30.00/$35.00

Oldsmobile 98
1955, 4"
(skirted fenders)
rare version
$30.00/$35.00/$40.00

Oldsmobile 98
1955, 4"
(open fenders)
1955 – 1960
$25.00/$30.00/$35.00

Oldsmobile 88 Convertible
1959, 6"
1960 – 1968
$15.00/$25.00/$35.00

Packard
4-door, 1956, 6"
1956 – 1959
$25.00/$35.00/$45.00

Packard
4-door, 1956, 6"
(tow hook)
1956 – 1959
$30.00/$40.00/$50.00

Packard
4-door, 1956, 6"
(tin bottom)
1956 – 1959
$55.00/$65.00/$75.00

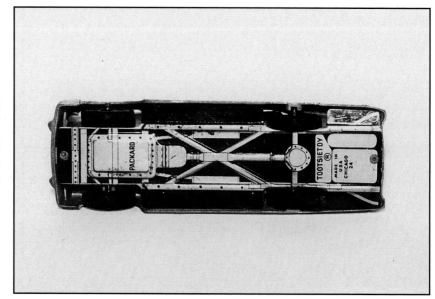

Plymouth
4-door, Sedan, 1950, 3"
1951 – 1954
$15.00/$20.00/$25.00

Plymouth
2-door, 1957, 3"
(1959 – 1969)
$12.00/$16.00/$20.00

Pontiac Sedan
1950, 4"
1950 – 1954
$25.00/$30.00/$35.00

Pontiac Sedan
1950, 4"
1950 – 1954
(rare two-tone)
$30.00/$35.00/$40.00

Thunderbird Coupe
1955, 3"
1955 – 1960
$15.00/$20.00/$25.00

Triumph TR 3 Roadster
1956, 3"
1963 – 1969
$12.00/$16.00/$20.00

VW Bug
1960, 3"
1960 – 1964
$12.00/$16.00/$20.00

VW Bug
1960, 6"
1960 – 1964
$25.00/$35.00/$45.00

Jeepster
1947, 3"
1949 – 1952
$20.00/$25.00/$30.00

CJ3 Civilian Jeep
1950, 3"
1952 – 1955, 1958 – 1961
$20.00/$25.00/$30.00

CJ3 Civilian Jeep
1947, 4"
1947 – 1954
(rubber tires)
1955 – 1969
(plastic tires)
$15.00/$20.00/$25.00

Racer
1949, 3"
1949 – 54
$20.00/$25.00/$30.00

Civilian Jeep
1949, 6"
(sold separate and in many sets)
$15.00/$25.00/$35.00

CJ5 Jeep, 1956, 6"
(windshield up)
1956 – 1959
$20.00/$25.00/$30.00

CJ5 Jeep, 1956, 6"
(windshield down)
1961
$25.00/$30.00/$35.00

CJ5 Jeep
1956, 6"
(with snowplow)
1961
(rare)
$35.00/$40.00/$45.00

BUSES, DOZERS, AND MISCELLANEOUS TOOTSIETOYS
(HO, MIDGET, AND CLASSIC SERIES)

Tootsietoy buses came in all sizes and shapes produced both before and after the war. The Jumbo series TransAmerica is the rarest bus to find for your collection. It came in red and silver and blue and silver. The Jumbo buses also came with a black tinplate bottom, which was often lost.

The small Midget Series Tootsietoys were produced from 1936 to 1941. They were packaged in two different ways — a small petitioned box and a small flat box with cutouts for the toys. The small game pieces and party favor assortments weren't considered midgets. Examples of the many Cracker Jack pieces and game pieces are pictured in this chapter.

The Classic Series was introduced in the early 1960s and had a short production until 1965. The 1921 Mack Dump was not sold with the other cars. It was sold separately and is really rare. Earlier models had gold plastic spoke-like wheels, but the Model A has solid plastic black wheels or tires.

The rare little four-inch pull wagon with its wire looped handle was sold in set No. 4615 in 1947. This toy is extremely scarce today. All of the pieces I have seen have been painted red with silver trim on the front of the toy.

The small little road signs and toy badges were items from different bagged toys and boxed sets.

The Corvair, Cadillac convertible, and Rambler wagon were all made by Lone Star, a company in England that produced the Matchbox looking models. I need the Ford Sunliner to complete this series of vehicles.

In 1932 Tootsietoy came out with a series called the Funnies Series which had a limited production run because at that time, they were not as popular as other models. The Funnies Series models were: Andy Gump, Uncle Walt, Smitty, Moon Mullins, KO Ice, and Uncle Willie. These pieces, if found at shows, will be priced at approximately $350.00 – $500.00. Do you know what a good return on the original boxed set No. 5091 containing all six pieces would bring? Remember, the set retailed for only $1.00 in 1932 catalogs.

If I missed anything other than the doll furniture that I mentioned in the introduction, please feel free to let me know. The new chapter now contains all Tractors and all HO series rare mini vans.

No. 4651
Fageol Bus
1927 – 1933
$45.00/$65.00/$85.00

No. 4654
Farm Tractor
1927 – 1932
$70.00/$110.00/$150.00

No. 4680
Overland Bus
1929 – 1933
(separate grill)
$75.00/$110.00/$145.00

Box Trailer
Roadscraper Set
1928 – 1932
$135.00/$185.00/$260.00

No. 4646
Caterpillar Tractor
1931 – 1939
(40s in sets only)
$25.00/$35.00/$50.00

No. 4648
Steamroller
1931 – 1934
$110.00/$160.00/$210.00

No. 5101X
Andy Gump
1932 – 1933
$375.00 – $475.00

No. 5102X
Uncle Walt
1932 – 1933
$375.00 – $475.00

No. 5103X
Smitty
1932 – 1933
$375.00 – $475.00

No. 5104X
Moon Mullins
1932 – 1933
$375.00 – $475.00

No. 5105X
KO Ice
1932 – 1933
$375.00 – $475.00

No. 5106X
Uncle Willie
1932 – 1933
$375.00 – $475.00

No. 4654
Army Tractor
1931 – 1932
(rare)
(Note: Ammo Box)
$80.00/$130.00/$170.00

No. 1045
Greyhound Bus
1937 – 1941
(made with and without
tin bottom)
$40.00/$55.00/$70.00

No. 1045
Greyhound Bus
1942 – 1946
$35.00/$50.00/$65.00

No. 3571
GMC Bus
1948 – 1955
$35.00/$50.00/$65.00

Twin Coach Bus
1949, 3"
1949 – 1950
$30.00/$40.00/$50.00

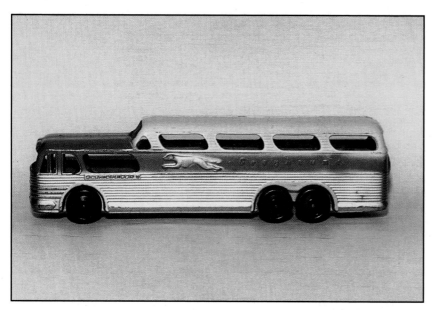

GMC Scenicruiser
1955, 7"
1955 – 1969
(plastic tires later models)
$25.00/$35.00/$40.00
NOTE: Early version had
a solid bottom.

No. 1910
Cat Bulldozer, 6"
(sold without blade also)
1956 – 1967
$30.00/$40.00/$50.00

No. 3710
Cat Scraper
1956, 5½"
1956 – 1959
(metal blade)
$35.00/$40.00/$45.00

No. 3710
Cat Scraper
1956, 5½"
1960 – 1967
(plastic blade)
$30.00/$35.00/$40.00

"TRANSAMERICA"
(Sets only 1941)
$150.00/$175.00/$200.00

HO Series
Ford & Rambler
1960s
$15.00/$20.00/$25.00

HO Series
Cadillac
1960s
$15.00/$20.00/$25.00

HO Series
No. 2470
Dump Truck
1960s
$25.00/$30.00/$45.00

HO Series
No. 2485
Tow Truck
1960s
$25.00/$30.00/$45.00

HO Series
No. 2490
School Bus
1960s
(scarce)
$35.00/$40.00/$45.00

HO Series
No. 2465 Metro
Milk, U.S. Mail
1960s
$35.00/$40.00/$45.00

HO Series
No. 2465 Metro
Dry Cleaners
Parcel Service
1960s
$35.00/$40.00/$45.00

HO Series
No. 2465 Metro
Railway Express
1960s
$35.00/$40.00/$45.00

Pull wagon with handle
1947, 4" (rare)
$65.00/$85.00/$105.00

Midget Series
1", 1936 – 1941
Stake Truck, Limo
Doodlebug, Railcar
Racer, Fire Truck
$9.00/$12.00/$15.00

Midget Series
1", 1936 – 1941
Cannon, Tank
Armored Car
Tow Truck
Camelback Van
$9.00/$12.00/$15.00

Midget Series
I", 1936 – 1941
(assorted ships)
$9.00/$12.00/$15.00

Midget Series
I", 1936 – 1941
Single Engine Plane
St. Louis, Bomber
Atlantic Clipper
$9.00/$12.00/$15.00

Assorted Road Signs
(signs from bagged toys)
Note: Signs not midgets
$4.00/$6.00/$8.00

Classic Series
1907 Stanley Steamer
1960 – 1965
$20.00/$25.00/$30.00

Classic Series
1912, Ford Model T
1960 – 1965
$20.00/$25.00/$30.00

Classic Series
1929 Ford Model A
1960 – 1965
$20.00/$25.00/$30.00

Classic Series
1919 Stutz Bearcat
1960 – 1965
$20.00/$25.00/$30.00

Classic Series
1906 Cadillac
1960 – 1965
$25.00/$30.00/$35.00

Classic Series
1921 Mack Dump
(years unknown)
1960?
(rare)
$30.00/$40.00/$50.00

Corvair, 1960
4" (English made)
1960 – 1961
$30.00/$40.00/$50.00

Rambler, 1960
4" (English made)
1960 – 1961
$30.00/$40.00/$50.00

Cadillac, 1960
4" (English made)
1960 – 1961
$35.00/$45.00/$55.00

No. 1011
Tractor
(1941 catalog only)
rare
$125.00/$145.00/$165.00

No. 2810
Tractor & Harrow
1952 – 1969
$45.00/$65.00/$75.00

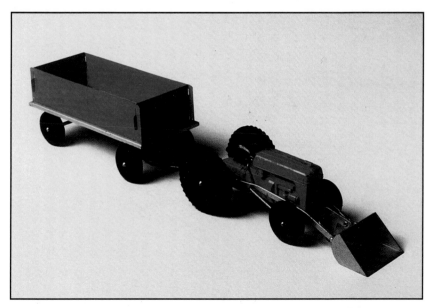

No. 290
Tractor with shovel and wagon
1953 – 1958
$115.00/$130.00/$145.00

Ford Tractor
(two-tone)
detailed motor
$35.00/$45.00/$55.00

Ford Tractor
(two-tone)
less detailed motor
spoked front wheels
$45.00/$55.00/$65.00

Ford Tractor
(cast seat & steering wheel)
$40.00/$50.00/$60.00

Badges
Deputy, Special Police
Fire Chief
G-man not shown
$10.00/$15.00/$20.00

Gas Pump Island
1960s
$30.00/$40.00/$50.00

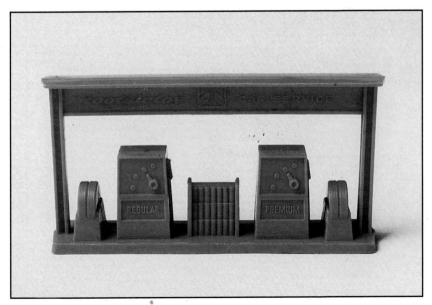

Gas Pump Island
(plastic)
1963 – 1966
$10.00/$15.00/$20.00

No. 895
Pontiac Safari Wagon
7", 1956 – 1958
$75.00/$150.00/$225.00

No. 995
Mercedes Benz 300 SL
7", 1956 – 1958
$100.00/$175.00/$250.00

Assorted game markers
$1.00/$2.00/$3.00

Baggage Cart Truck and Ramp
$25.00/$30.00/$35.00

United Airlines
Wing Badges
$15.00/$20.00/$25.00

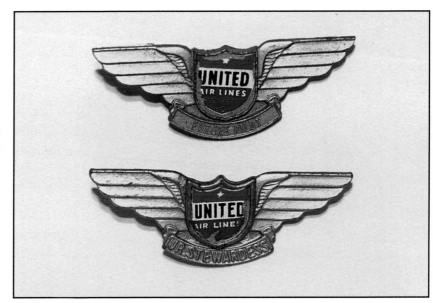

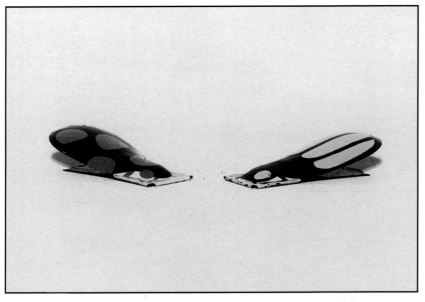

Dowst Cluckers
1936
No Price Available

GENERAL MOTORS SERIES
1927 – 1933

This group of toy cars and screen-sided vans had six basic body styles, which were interchangeable on four styles of chassis. The combinations made up 24 different models each having its own catalog number.

The six different bodies styles were: Coupe, Roadster, Brougham, Sedan, Touring Car Sedan, and a detailed Screenside Delivery Van. The chassis types were the Chevrolet, Buick, Oldsmobile, Cadillac, and later no-name types.

In the series, late in 1933, a nameless model was made of each body type. The radiator grills were without any raised lettering like other models in the series. These vehicles had the optional white rubber tires on a small cast rim instead of the disc wheel tire combination. Wheels of this type were later used on the 1934 Ford series 3" toys and various Mack Army 3" models.

Gold painted disc wheels appeared on 1927 and 1928 models of that era. Wheels were painted black from 1929 through 1933, the only exception being some later 1932 and 1933 pieces that had the small white rubber tires on cast rims.

I tend to agree with my fellow authors and collector friends that the Buicks are the most common in the series and the nameless would be more difficult to obtain for a complete collection.

The hardest and last body type for my own collection was the open Tourer with its top up. The nicely colored photos in this section will better illustrate to you some of the many color schemes used on this great series of automobiles and panel delivery vans.

Examples in this series can be purchased at local toy shows from $45.00 to way over $100.00 depending on condition of the toy and your state or locale. Many of these ten cent toys are still available to the collector. Have fun collecting this complete series with its nicely colored toys. These will make a fine addition to anyone's Tootsietoy collection.

Examples in the photos that follow are all original toys that have not been restored.

CATALOG NUMBERS

No. 6001   Buick Roadster – $45.00/$60.00/$75.00
No. 6002   Buick Coupe – $40.00/$50.00/$60.00
No. 6003   Buick Brougham – $40.00/$50.00/$60.00
No. 6004   Buick Sedan – $40.00/$50.00/$60.00
No. 6005   Buick Touring (closed) – $45.00/$65.00/$75.00
No. 6101   Cadillac Roadster – $45.00/$85.00/$125.00
No. 6102   Cadillac Coupe – $45.00/$85.00/$125.00
No. 6103   Cadillac Brougham – $45.00/$85.00/$125.00
No. 6104   Cadillac Sedan – $45.00/$85.00/$125.00
No. 6105   Cadillac Touring (closed) – $80.00/$105.00/$130.00
No. 6201   Chevrolet Roadster – $45.00/$60.00/$75.00
No. 6202   Chevrolet Coupe – $45.00/$60.00/$75.00
No. 6203   Chevrolet Brougham – $45.00/$60.00/$75.00
No. 6204   Chevrolet Sedan – $45.00/$60.00/$75.00
No. 6205   Chevrolet Touring (closed) – $110.00/$160.00/$210.00
No. 6301   Oldsmobile Roadster – $45.00/$60.00/$75.00
No. 6302   Oldsmobile Coupe – $45.00/$60.00/$75.00
No. 6303   Oldsmobile Bougham – $45.00/$60.00/$75.00
No. 6304   Oldsmobile Sedan – $45.00/$60.00/$75.00
No. 6305   Oldsmobile Touring (closed) – $75.00/$115.00/$150.00
No. 6-01   Roadster – $80.00/$110.00/$135.00
No. 6-02   Coupe – $80.00/$110.00/$135.00
No. 6-03   Brougham – $80.00/$110.00/$135.00
No. 6-04   Sedan – $80.00/$110.00/$135.00
No. 6-05   Touring (closed) – $110.00/$150.00/$190.00
No. 6006   Buick Delivery Van – $60.00/$85.00/$115.00
No. 6106   Cadillac Delivery Van – $50.00/$90.00/$130.00
No. 6206   Chevrolet Delivery Van – $50.00/$70.00/$90.00
No. 6306   Oldsmobile Delivery Van – $110.00/$160.00/$210.00

Photo showing various grill fronts.

Roadster

Coupe

Sedan

Brougham

Tourer
(rare)

Delivery Van

TOOTSIETOY GRAHAMS
1933 – 1939

Dowst Manufacturing Company introduced the Graham series in its new line-up for 1933. It included the Grahams in all their new colors and great detail with nickel-plated shiny grill fronts. The two-piece bodies of basically eight styles were mounted on several different chassis designs.

The body types were Coupe, Sedan, Wrecker, Ambulance, Roadster, Town Car, Dairy Van, and the limited production Commercial Tire Van.

There are two basic methods in which the Grahams were put together. One is the "BUILD-A-CAR" sets by which divided axles, held by small clips in the center, connected the body to the chassis. The other type has a long nail passing through the wheel centers, going through the body lower loops, and being crimped on the passenger side of the toy, thus locking the body to the chassis.

Several actual Graham models never really existed in any of their catalogs. These included the Town Car without spare tire, Panel Vans with side spares, Station Wagon, and a Mail Truck Van. In the event you may encounter one of these odd balls, it was probably the result of some chopper or child's father trying to put together a one-of-a-kind toy for his child. There are, however, many minor variations of castings including body, chassis, grills, and wheels. It is almost impossible to date or pinpoint the exact years.

The convertible Coupes and Sedans were merely two-tone cars with a painted roof. A light khaki paint was applied to the roof to simulate the convertible top's being up on the toy. These models have their own catalog numbers as well.

In 1937 the Commercial Tire Van replaced the Roadster in boxed set No. 5360 BUILD-A-CAR set or BILD-A-CAR as spelled in Tootsietoy catalogs. The Commercial Tire Van carries the high price tag of $200.00 or more if you are lucky to find a nice example of this toy for sale.

Endless color combinations can be found in the BILD-A-CAR sets, TAXI boxed sets, and on individually packaged Grahams. There are over 100 different color combinations in all for the eight body types.

Happy collecting and good luck hunting these rascals down. Examples of body types with their catalog number will follow. Most of the toys pictured are original with a couple restored ones painted their original color schemes with new tires added.

Graham Sedan (Taxi Set)
$95.00 – $115.00

Graham Coupe (BILD-A-CAR set)
$95.00 – $115.00

0511 Graham
5 Wheel Roadster
$125.00 – $150.00 (mint)

0512 Graham
5 Wheel Coupe
$125.00 – $150.00 (mint)

0513 Graham
5 Wheel Sedan
$125.00 – $150.00 (mint)

0514 Graham
5 Wheel Convertible Coupe
$125.00 – $150.00 (mint)

0515 Graham
5 Wheel Convertible Sedan
$125.00 – $150.00 (mint)

0516 Graham
5 Wheel Town Car
$125.00 – $150.00 (mint)

0611 Graham
6 Wheel Roadster
$140.00 – $170.00 (mint)

0612 Graham
6 Wheel Coupe
$125.00 – $150.00 (mint)

0613 Graham
6 Wheel Sedan
$125.00 – $150.00 (mint)

0614 Graham
6 Wheel Convertible Coupe
$125.00 – $150.00 (mint)

0615 Graham
6 Wheel Convertible Sedan
$125.00 – $150.00 (mint)

0616 Graham
6 Wheel Town Car
$125.00 – $150.00 (mint)

0809 Graham
Ambulance
$75.00/$100.00/$125.00

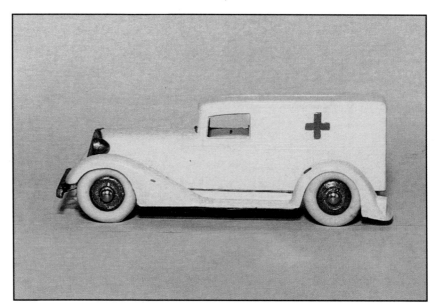

0809 Graham
Ambulance
(Army)
$85.00/$110.00/$135.00

0808 Graham
Dairy Van
$125.00/$150.00/$175.00

No number
Commercial Tire
(sets only)
$135.00/$160.00/$225.00

0806 Graham Wrecker
$80.00/$90.00/$100.00

Graham BILD-A-CAR
(bottom view)
$75.00 – $100.00 (mint)
NOTE: Small sleeves
center of axles.

MILITARY ITEMS

Tootsietoy, like its competitors of the early 1930s and 1950s, produced some very nice detailed toys. The No. 4643 Mack Gun Truck and No. 4644 Searchlight Truck were all produced with different wheel types and paint schemes. The small black die-steel wheels are the most common type. Miniature white rubber tires mounted on separate rims would be the rarest of the three. The same type of wheel was also used on the 1934 Ford 3" cars. The last type is a solid white rubber tire produced from 1935 till around 1941.

The many military vehicle types can be found in solid colors or the very nice camouflaged paint schemes. Postwar production brought back many familiar pieces from the pre-war years. Different tires were the most obvious changes. Tires were replaced with a black rubber tire for better wear.

In the 1950s and early 1960s many of the pieces were sold in boxed sets, blister packages, and separately boxed toys. Several sets contained a plastic soldier or two along with other military vehicles. Like all original boxed sets, be prepared to pay a lot more than the actual values listed for individual pieces in my guide. Very few examples exist and they are rarely for sale in today's toy market.

The Army Jeeps of all three sizes are quite easy to purchase for your collection. The only real exception is the CJ5 Military Jeep with its yellow snow plow. Several items are on the rare list like the Army Radar Trailer, 155mm Howitzer Tank, and the 1955 RC 180 Army or Navy Rocket Launcher and rocket trucks. Separate models are located hereafter.

No. 4642, Long Range Cannon, 1931 – 1940
$15.00/$20.00/$25.00

No. 4643
Mack Anti-Aircraft Gun
1931
$35.00/$45.00/$55.00

No. 4644
Mack Searchlight
1931
$35.00/$45.00/$55.00

No. 4643
Mack Anti-Aircraft Gun
1940
$30.00/$40.00/$50.00

Army Half Track
1941 (1960)
$25.00/$30.00/$35.00

No. 4635
Armored Car
1946 – 1948
$25.00/$35.00/$45.00

No. 4635
Armored Car
1946 – 1948
$25.00/$35.00/$45.00

No. 4647
Army Tank (Renault)
1931 – 1941
$45.00/$55.00/$65.00

No. 4635
Armored Car
1938
$35.00/$45.00/$55.00

No. 4634
Army Supply Truck
1939
$55.00/$65.00/$75.00

CJ3 Army Jeep
1950, 3"
1955
Note: no cast steering
wheel on dashboard
$15.00/$20.00/$25.00

CJ3 Army Jeep
1947, 4"
$20.00/$25.00/$30.00

CJ3 Army Jeep
1950, 3"
1958
$10.00/$15.00/$20.00

Chevy Ambulance
1950, 4"
$25.00/$30.00/$35.00

Ford F700 Army Stake
1956, 6"
$50.00/$65.00/$80.00

Ford F700 Army Radar
1956, 6"
$40.00/$45.00/$50.00

Ford F700 Searchlight
1956, 6"
$50.00/$65.00/$80.00

Ford F700 Army Anti-Aircraft Gun
1956, 6"
$40.00/$45.00/$50.00

Four Wheel Cannon
1950s, 4"
$15.00/$20.00/$25.00

Army Tank
1958 – 1960
$15.00/$20.00/$25.00

Army Searchlight
1950s, 3"
$25.00/$30.00/$35.00

Six Wheel Army Cannon
1950s, 4"
$20.00/$25.00/$30.00

Army Radar Trailer
1959 – 1960 (rare)
$40.00/$45.00/$50.00

155mm Howitzer
1958 – 1960
$60.00/$75.00/$90.00

Oldsmobile Staff Car
1958 – 1960, 4"
$30.00/$35.00/$40.00

4I International Ambulance
1949
$40.00/$45.00/$50.00

Modern Field Cannon
1958 – 1960
$15.00/$20.00/$25.00

RC 180 Lowboy Trailer
1965
$45.00/$55.00/$65.00

CJ5 Army Jeep
1956
$15.00/$20.00/$25.00

CJ5 Army Jeep
(Windshield down)
1961
$20.00/$25.00/$30.00

CJ5 Army Jeep
with snowplow
1961
$30.00/$40.00/$50.00

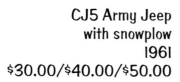

Tootsietoy Soldiers
1938
$30.00/$40.00/$50.00
NOTE: Flag bearer
not pictured.

RC 180 Army Rocket Launcher
1958 – 1960
$105.00/$120.00/$135.00

Army Jeep
1950s, 6"
(all wheel types)
$20.00/$25.00/$30.00

PACKAGED TOYS AND BOXED SETS

Packaged toys and boxed sets of Tootsietoys are very hard to obtain. The first type of packaging used was a small plastic or cellophane-like bag. The toy or toys were put in the bag and stapled at the top. A small hole was punched in the bag top so it could be hung on the various types of counter displays and free standing vertical display racks.

The next form of packaging was the most common blister pack. The toy or toys were placed on a colorful cardboard backing with a heavy plastic placed on top of the toy and heated, thus sealing the toy airtight. A small cardboard box with the toy clearly illustrated on the outside and a catalog number on the two end flaps of the box was the third type of packaging.

Boxed sets are probably the most popular with collectors of all the various packaging. As a rule, you could add 20% or more to the boxed set of pieces depending on condition of the box in which they were originally packaged.

I have included many examples of packaging and some boxed sets that I have in my collection along with examples from several friends who were kind enough to allow me to photograph them. All photos in this chapter are new items and not found in my previous book.

Happy Collecting!

No. 170
Interchangeable Truck Set (1928)
1925 – 1931
$200.00

117

No. 2935
Army Jeep
Cannon, 3 Men
1960, 1963
$65.00

1962 Ford Wagon
Boat Trailer, Boat
1962 – 1968
$100.00

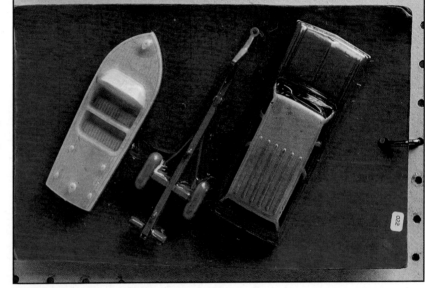

No. 2906
Pontiac, Cameo
Pickup, Chrysler & Ramp
1963
$110.00

No. 2912
62 Ford Econoline, Trailer, Bull,
and Cowboy
1963 – 1965
$100.00

No. 2825
62 Ford Wagon,
U-Haul & Tire Load
1962 – 1968
$65.00

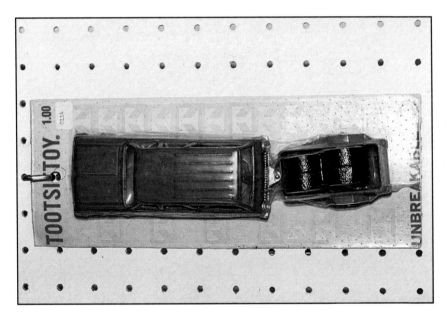

No. 2901
55 Mack B,
Utility Trailer & Animals
1960 – 1961
$125.00

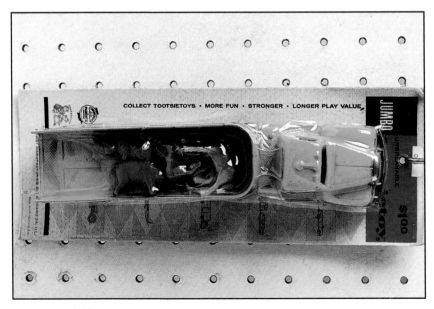

COLLECT TOOTSIETOYS · MORE FUN · STRONGER · LONGER PLAY VALUE

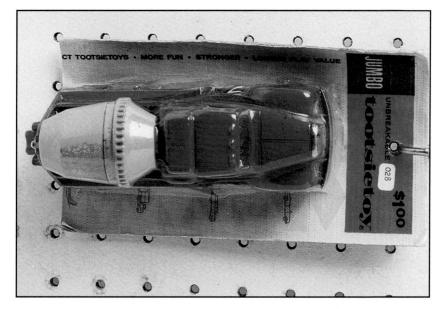

No. 2945
55 Mack B
Cement, worm axle
1960 – 1961
$75.00
NOTE: First type of axle.

No. 2460
HO Rambler &
Ford Convertible
1960 – 1962
$60.00

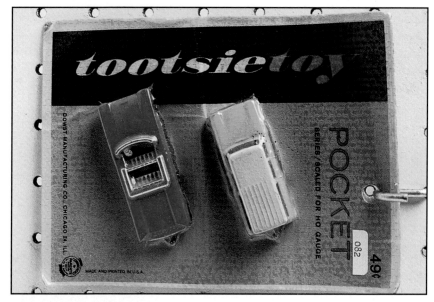

MINIATURES: Hat, Top,
Clicker, Iron, Etc.
1959 – 1960
$65.00

1956 Cameo, 4 Tools
1956 – 1958
$60.00

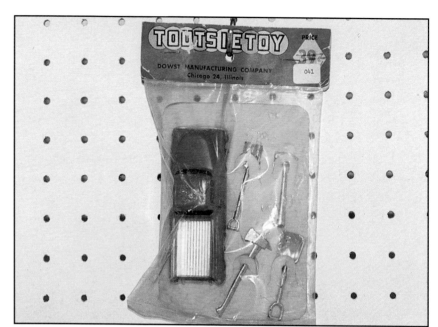

No. 2310
54 Ford Wagon,
Badge, and Whistle
1959 – 1960
$55.00

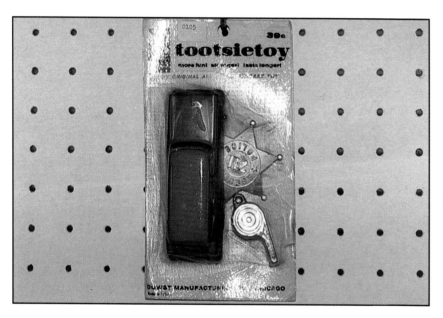

No. 2400
Military Field
Cannon and plastic shells (rare)
1959
Navy blue
$40.00

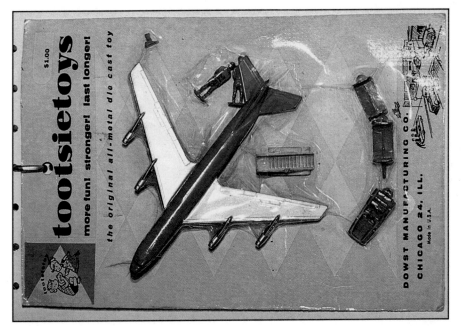

No. 2941
Boeing 707 Jet, Loading Ramp,
Carts, and Baggage Truck
1960 – 1961, 1964 – 1966
$110.00

No. 4210
Land and Air
1959
$300.00

No. 5211
Tootsietoy Fire Department
1953 – 1955
$500.00

1950 Chevy Panel
with Road Sign
1956 – 1958
$45.00

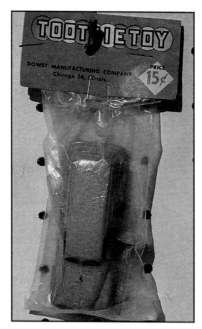

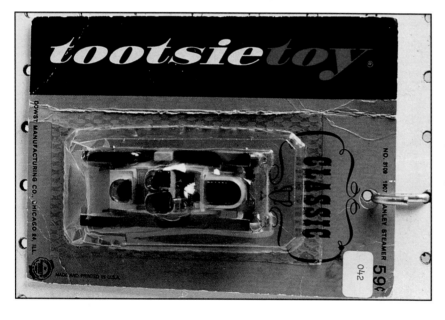

No. 3109
907 Stanley Steamer
1960 – 1965
$35.00

50 Chevy Ambulance,
Badge, and Gun
1956 – 1958
$60.00

No. 4335
Tootsietoy Camping Set
1963
$325.00

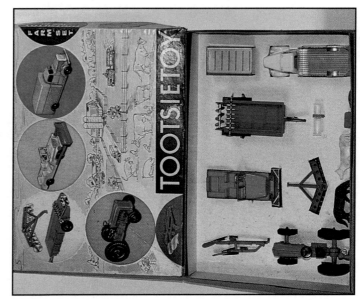

No. 6800
Farm Set
1958
$375.00

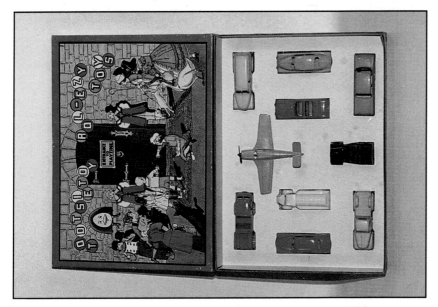

No. 5149
Highway Set
1952 – 1953
$350.00

No. 4700
Highway Set, 1949
$350.00

Caterpillar Scraper with box, 1956
$75.00

SHIPS

The Tootsietoy all-metal ships were introduced in the catalogs around 1940. There are ten different models. The ships are very fragile with their tiny cast guns, masts, flags, and airplanes on the No. 1036 Carrier and one plane on the No. 1035 Cruiser.

The all-metal ships actually came in two series of paint styles. Series one ships, which are much more common, are silver and red military and multicolor commercial vessels. The second series in 1941 and 1942 are gray and red, or the English type camouflage like No. 129 Tender pictured in this chapter.

Tootsietoy ships, like all other Tootsietoys, now are really getting hard to find in mint condition. I've seen some boxed sets of the war ships at shows priced more than double the price of the pieces themselves.

Ships of the 1970s are located in the chapter on Tootsietoys 1970 – 1979. The small 1" and 2" ships of the Midget Series are located in the Buses, Dozers, and Miscellaneous Tootsietoys chapter.

Collecting all ten ships in series one and series two paint schemes would be a challenge to any collector. I have been very fortunate to upgrade almost all my ships this past year.

The Tootsietoy all-metal ships were under valued in my revised value guide of 1993 and also other value guides. My new prices take into consideration the rarity of mint pieces and also take an average of show selling prices. Happy hunting!

No. 1034 Battleship
$20.00/$25.00/$30.00

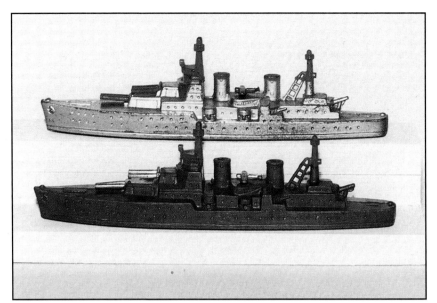

No. 1035 Cruiser
$20.00/$25.00/$30.00

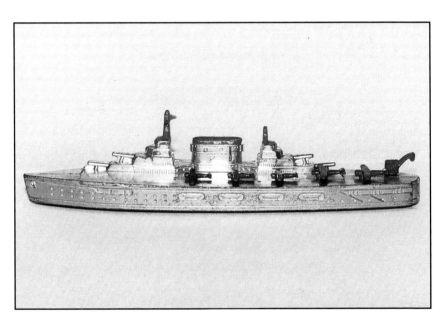

No. 1036 Carrier
$25.00/$30.00/$35.00

No. 1037 Transport
$20.00/$25.00/$30.00

No. 1038 Freighter
$20.00/$25.00/$30.00

No. 1039 Tanker
$20.00/$25.00/$30.00

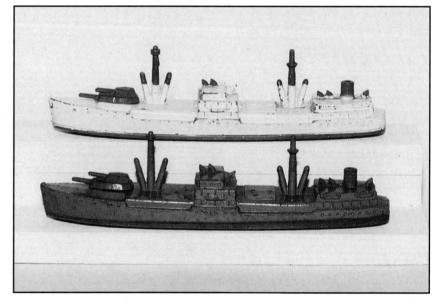

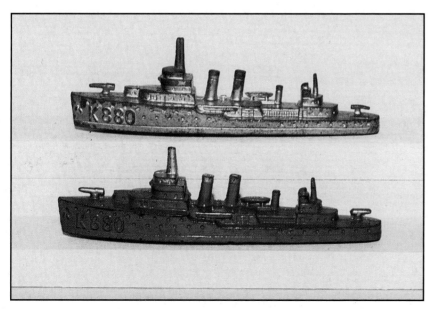

No. 127 Destroyer
$15.00/$20.00/$25.00

No. 128 Submarine
$15.00/$20.00/$25.00

No. 129 Tender
(English camouflage)
$20.00/$25.00/$30.00

No. 130 Yacht
$25.00/$30.00/$35.00

TRAILERS

Besides the Huber box trailer of the earlier years and the many cannons and military type trailers, others were produced to be pulled by vehicles — a 1937 Tootsietoy catalog pictures the No. 1043 small house trailer and No. 1044 Roamer trailer. The small camping or house trailer was always sold with a 1935 Ford 3" sedan that was the same color as the trailer. I've seen sets in red, blue, green, and silver (the most common). The No. 1044 Roamer trailer was designed for use with the La Salle Coupe and Sedan. It has a floor plate and sliding door through which it can be loaded. It was sold singly only in 1937, later only in set No. 180. The Roamer trailer by far is the rarest pre-war trailer.

Both 4" and 6" post-war trailers were usually packaged with a 6" car or pickup truck. Assorted trailers also help to make up several different camping sets. These include the different boat, house, horse, race car, and U-haul trailers. The restaurant and the 4½" Stake Trailer of 1963 are the hardest two trailers to obtain for your collection. A yellow Stake Trailer is pictured in this chapter, but missing its brown plastic stake-like tailgate. A packaged toy complete with Ford Econoline pickup truck is pictured in Packaged Toys chapter.

Many other trailers are pictured in the 1970s chapter.

No. 1044 Roamer Trailer
1937 – 1939
$150.00/$175.00/$200.00

Small House Trailer
1937 – 1939
$25.00/$40.00/$55.00

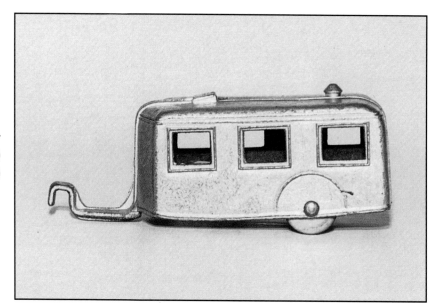

Horse Trailer
1961 – 1965
$10.00/$15.00/$20.00

U-Haul Trailer
1958 – 1961
$10.00/$15.00/$20.00

House Trailer
1960 – 1967
$15.00/$20.00/$25.00

Boat Trailer
1959 – 1963
$15.00/$20.00/$25.00

Restaurant Trailer
(Refreshment sign
top is missing.)
1960 – 1961, 1963
$35.00/$45.00/$55.00

Stake Trailer (missing tailgate)
1963
$20.00/$30.00/$40.00

Race Car Trailer
1960 – 1961, 1963 – 1968
$20.00/$25.00/$30.00

TRAINS

The first tootsietoy train, I believe, was the No. 4397 set produced in 1921. It consisted of an engine with a large smoke stack, tender, and two coaches finished in a beautiful silver-plate finish. I have never had a chance to see even a photo of this very rare train.

The 1932 catalog shows us many different freight and passenger trains. Many of the trains were produced in boxed sets, and separate pieces of train cars and engines were sold so a young child could construct a train with as many cars as he or she wanted. The No. 7002 Fast Freight Set consisted of a locomotive, tender, box-car, gondola car, and a caboose, usually painted in bright colors. The No. 7002 set was repackaged and numbered No. 194 from 1932 – 1937. The Midnight Flyer Set No. 7001 was the passenger set of the same era. It consisted of a baggage car, pullman car, and an observation car at the end. They were painted a light pastel yellow, red, green, or blue. Engines and tenders of both trains above were always painted black. Set No. 7001 was also repackaged and renumbered as No. 193 from 1932 – 1937.

The year 1937 brought a totally new train, No. 196. This was a streamlined train consisting of three pieces in total. The train was a copy of the Union Pacific Flyer streamliner. I have this train in silver and also two-toned red and silver in my own personal collection. I am told that a blue and silver version of this train exists also. The fall of 1937 brought still another new arrival to the already growing line of Tootsietoy trains — the Broadway Limited, a copy of that popular New York/Chicago train. The snub-nosed engine had Pennsylvania clearly marked on its tender in raised lettering. Engine and tender cars were cast in one piece for this new No. 188 set. To better distinguish the engine from others, it also carried number 5435 under the engine windows.

The years 1939 – 1941 brought the ever-popular No. 1086 Pennsylvania and No. 1076 Santa Fe Locomotives with nine different cars to build upon your engine and tender cars. All the cars were 5¼" in length. The only exceptions are the engine at 6" and the small caboose at 3¼" in length. Examples of engines and nine different cars are pictured in this chapter.

The Fast Freight set No. 186 issued around 1940 consisted of an engine, tender, and three cars. This set was sold in a long narrow colorful box. The Cracker Jack boxcar really makes this set highly collectible.

I do not have any information about the diesel train sets produced around 1955 at this time. Any comments or information about Tootsietoy trains or sets is most welcomed.

No. 7001 Set or
later No. 193 Set
(Same pieces just
different numbers)
1932 – 1937
$90.00/$100.00/$110.00

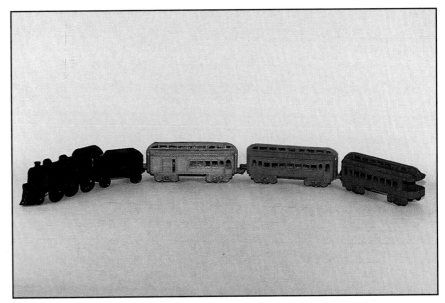

Passenger Train Set

No. 7002 Set or later
No. 194 Set
(Same pieces just
different numbers)
1932 – 1937
$110.00/$120.00/$130.00

Freight Train Set

No. 117 Zephyr Railcar
1935, 4" (rare)
1935 – 1936
$65.00/$85.00/$105.00

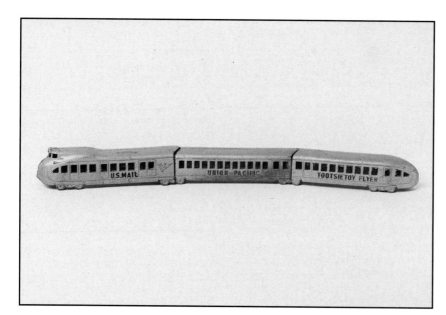

No. 196 Tootsietoy Flyer
1937 – 1941
Note: sold separately
and in many boxed sets.
$75.00/$100.00/$125.00

No. 196 Tootsietoy Flyer
1937 – 1941
(rare two-tone train)
$95.00/$120.00/$145.00

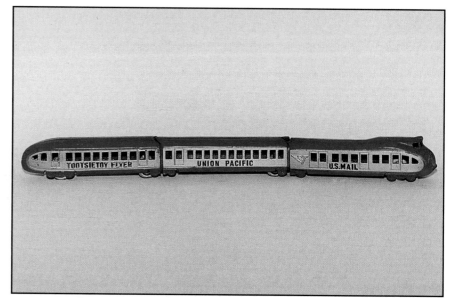

No. 1076 Santa Fe
No. 1086 Pennsylvania
1939 – 1941
$20.00/$25.00/$30.00

No. 1094 Oil Tank Car
$10.00/$15.00/$20.00

No. 1093 Milk Tank Car
$10.00/$15.00/$20.00

No. 1088 Refrigerator Car
$10.00/$15.00/$20.00

No. 1089 Box Car
(black rubber tires)
$10.00/$15.00/$20.00

No. 1092 Log Car
$15.00/$20.00/$25.00

No. 1087 Wrecking Crane
$15.00/$20.00/$25.00

No. 1091 Stock Car
$10.00/$15.00/$20.00

No. 1089 Box Car
$10.00/$15.00/$20.00

No. 1090 Coal Car
$10.00/$15.00/$20.00

No. 1095 Caboose
Note: green or red
$15.00/$20.00/$25.00

No. 188 Broadway
Limited Set, 1937
$120.00/$150.00/$170.00

No. 5851 Santa Fe
Limited Train Set
1941
Note: one Pullman car missing.
$125.00/$165.00/$200.00

No. 186 Fast Freight Set
1940 – 1941
$100.00/$125.00/$150.00

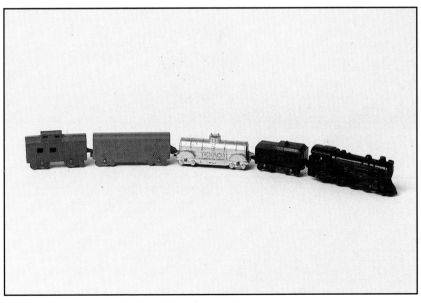

TRUCKS AND SEMIS

Strombecker Corporation has produced thousands of trucks, vans, and tractor trailer combinations. The first truck appeared in the 1916 catalog No. 4610 Model T pickup with its tiny shiny gold spoked wheels. Spoked wheels were replaced by solid discs in 1924.

The Federal 3" Grocery, Market, Bakery, Laundry, Milk, and Florist vans appeared around 1924 and were last seen in the 1933 catalog. The Florist is the rarest of this group. In 1925 special Federals were produced for different department stores and businesses. Some names were BOGGS & BUHL, POMEROY'S, WATT & SHAND, J.C. PENNEY, and more. Sorry to say at this time I do not have these in my collection to photograph for you.

Ever-popular Mack 3" trucks were made in 1924 and first appeared without a chain drive at the rear and with an M on the hood for Mack. A Stake, Coal, and Oil were made both with and without chain drives cast by the rear axle. The Mail truck was produced between 1931 and 1933 and is the rarest of this short series.

The first set of two Mack trucks and trailers appeared around 1929. This was set No. 4670 containing an A & P Trailer and American Railway Express each with its own cab. The 1933 catalog showed the Mack Domaco Oil, Express, Moving Van, City Fuel, and Dairy, plus others. Examples with single axle trailers and single axle trailers with dual tires on one axle are pictured in this chapter with all the other great looking Macks. My favorite would be the No. 187 Transport with three No. 230 series automobiles that was only in the catalog for one year — 1941. Someday I would like to take a survey and see just how many of these No. 187 sets exist today.

Tootsietoy pre-war examples are harder to locate than most of the post-war trucks and trailers. The two most common 4" trucks were the Stake and Oil 1949 Fords. These trucks were in catalogs from 1949 – 1969, the longest production of any other Tootsietoy truck pictured in my value guide.

No. 4610 Model T Pickup, 1914, 3", 1916 – 1923
$30.00/$45.00/$60.00

No. 4610 Model T Pickup
1914, 3"
1924 – 1932
$30.00/$40.00/$50.00

No. 0801
Mack Stake Trailer
1933 – 1935
$75.00/$90.00/$110.00

No. 0801
Mack Stake Trailer
1935 – 1941
$65.00/$80.00/$100.00

No. 0802
Mack Oil Trailer
1933 – 1935
$75.00/$90.00/$110.00

No. 0802
Mack Oil Trailer
1935 – 1939
$65.00/$80.00/$100.00

No. 0804
Mack Coal Truck
1933 – 1936
(dual axle)
$85.00/$115.00/$145.00

No. 0804
Mack Coal Truck
1937 – 1941
(single axle)
$75.00/$105.00/$135.00

No. 0805
Mack Milk Truck
1933 – 1935
(dual tires)
$85.00/$115.00/$145.00

No. 0805
Mack Milk Truck
1927 – 1939
(single tire)
$75.00/$105.00/$135.00

No. 0803
Mack Van Trailer
1933 – 1936
$80.00/$110.00/$140.00

No. 0192
Mack Milk Trailers
1933 – 1941
(3 trailers)
$110.00/$160.00/$210.00

No. 0191
Contractor Set
1933 – 1941
$100.00/$125.00/$150.00

No. 0190
Mack Transport
(Shown with three Buick cars)
1931 – 1933
$130.00/$150.00/$170.00

No. 0190X
Mack Transport
(Shown with four Buick cars)
1933 – 1936
$160.00/$180.00/$210.00

No. 198
Auto Transport
(Shown with three Ford cars)
1935 – 1941
$160.00/$180.00/$210.00

No. 0810
Mack Wrigley's Gum
1935 – 1941
$80.00/$115.00/$150.00

No. 0807
Delivery Cycle
1933
$105.00/$120.00/$135.00

No. 187
Mack Transport
1941 (rare)
$150.00/$190.00/$230.00

Federal Van
Grocery
1924 - 1933
$75.00/$100.00/$125.00

Federal
Laundry Van
1924 - 1933
$75.00/$100.00/$125.00

Federal Van
Milk
1924 - 1933
$65.00/$90.00/$115.00

Federal Van
Market
1924 – 1933
$75.00/$100.00/$125.00

Federal Van
Florist
1924 – 1933
(rare)
$125.00/$175.00/$200.00

No. 4638
Mack Stake, 1928
1928 – 1933
$55.00/$65.00/$75.00

No. 4639
Mack Coal, 1925
1925 – 1928
$55.00/$65.00/$75.00

No. 4639
Mack Coal, 1928
1928 – 1933
$50.00/$60.00/$70.00

No. 4640
Mack Oil, 1925
1925 – 1928
$50.00/$60.00/$70.00

No. 4645
Mack Mail
1931 – 1933
$55.00/$75.00/$95.00

No. 4652
Fire Hook & Ladder
1927 – 1933
$55.00/$75.00/$95.00

No. 4653
Fire Watertower Truck
1927 – 1933
$65.00/$85.00/$105.00

No. 4670
Mack Trailers
1929 – 1932
(rare)
$110.00/$125.00/$140.00

Unnumbered
Model A Mail, 1928
1931 – 1933
(sold in sets only)
$70.00/$85.00/$100.00

No. 0133
Ford Wrecker, 1934, 3"
1934 – 1935
$65.00/$75.00/$85.00

151

No. 0133
Ford Wrecker, 1935, 3"
1935 – 1941
$50.00/$60.00/$70.00

No. 0120
Oil Tanker
1936 – 1939
$50.00/$60.00/$70.00

No. 0121
Ford Pickup
1936, 3"
1936 – 1939
$55.00/$65.00/$75.00

No. 0123
Special Delivery
1936, 3"
1937 – 1939
$60.00/$70.00/$80.00

No. 1006
Standard Oil, 6"
1939 – 1941
$40.00/$55.00/$70.00

No. 1006
Standard Oil, 6"
1947
$35.00/$50.00/$65.00

1007
Sinclair Oil, 6"
1939 – 1941
$40.00/$55.00/$70.00

No. 1007
Sinclair Oil, 6"
1947
$35.00/$50.00/$65.00

No. 1008
Texaco Oil, 6"
1939 – 1941
$45.00/$60.00/$75.00

No. 1008
Texaco Oil, 6"
1947
$40.00/$55.00/$70.00

No. 1009
Shell Oil, 6"
1939 – 1941
$45.00/$60.00/$75.00

No. 1009
Shell Oil, 6"
1947
$40.00/$55.00/$70.00

No. 1010
Wrigley's Box Van
1940 – 1941
$70.00/$95.00/$105.00

No. 1010
Box Van, 4"
1948
$50.00/$75.00/$85.00

No. 1019
Jumbo Pickup
1936 – 1941
$35.00/$45.00/$55.00

No. 1019
Jumbo Pickup, 6"
1942, 1946
30.00/$40.00/$50.00

No. 1027
Jumbo Wrecker, 6"
1937 – 1941
$45.00/$55.00/$65.00

No. 1027
Jumbo Wrecker, 6"
1942, 1946
$40.00/$50.00/$60.00

No. 1040
Hook & Ladder, 4"
1937 – 1941
$60.00/$70.00/$80.00

No. 1041
Hose Car
1937 – 1941
$55.00/$65.00/$75.00

No. 1042
Insurance Patrol
1937 – 1941
$55.00/$65.00/$75.00

No. 234
Box Truck, 3"
1940 – 1941
$15.00/$20.00/$25.00

No. 234
Box Truck, 3"
1947 – 1948
$15.00/$20.00/$25.00

No. 235
Oil Tanker, 3"
(two caps top)
1940 – 1941
$15.00/$20.00/$25.00

No. 235
Oil Tanker, 3"
(two caps top)
1947 – 1948
$15.00/$20.00/$25.00

No. 235
Oil Tanker, 3"
(four caps post-war)
1947 – 1954
$15.00/$20.00/$25.00

No. 236
Hook & Ladder, 3"
1940 – 1941
(rare)
$40.00/$50.00/$60.00

No. 237
Insurance Patrol, 3"
1940 – 1941
$30.00/$40.00/$50.00

No. 238
Hose Wagon, 3"
1940 – 1941
$25.00/$35.00/$45.00

No. 238
Hose Wagon, 3"
1947 – 1948
$25.00/$35.00/$45.00

American La France
Pumper, 1949, 3"
1949 – 1959
$15.00/$20.00/$25.00

American La France
Pumper, 1949, 3"
1949 – 1959
(Note: axles put inside fenders)
$15.00/$20.00/$25.00

Chevy Cameo Pickup
1956, 4"
1959 – 1969
$20.00/$25.00/$30.00

Chevy Panel
1950, 4"
1950 – 1953
$25.00/$35.00/$45.00

Chevy Panel
1950, 4"
(two-tone)
1950 – 1953
$30.00/$40.00/$50.00

Chevy Ambulance
1950, 4"
1953 – 1960
$30.00/$40.00/$50.00

Chevy Panel, 1950, 3"
(open & closed rear windows)
1950 – 1959
$15.00/$20.00/$25.00

Chevy Panel, 1950, 3"
(open & closed rear windows)
1950 – 1959
Note: front fenders
$15.00/$20.00/$25.00

Chevy El Camino
1950, 6"
1960 – 1967
$25.00/$35.00/$45.00

Chevy El Camino
Camper and Boat
1962 – 1964
$55.00/$65.00/$75.00

Dodge Panel, 1956, 6"
1959 – 1966
Without tin bottom:
$35.00/$50.00/$65.00
With tin bottom:
$55.00/$75.00/$95.00

Dodge Pickup, 1950, 4"
1950 – 1960
(open small windows)
$20.00/$25.00/$30.00

Dodge Pickup, 1950, 4"
1950 – 1960
(closed small windows)
$20.00/$25.00/$30.00

Hudson Pickup,
1947, 4"
(rare)
1947 – 1949
$35.00/$45.00/$55.00

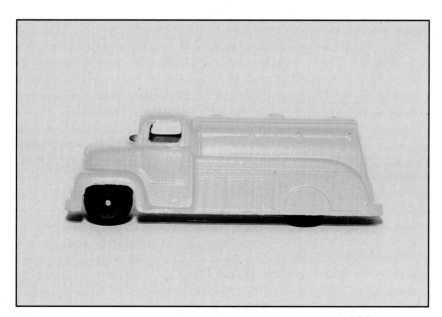

Ford C600 Oil, 3"
1955 – 1960
$15.00/$20.00/$25.00

Ford C600 Oil
1962, 6"
1962 – 1966
$15.00/$20.00/$25.00

Ford Econoline Pickup
1962, 6"
1962 – 1969
$20.00/$25.00/$30.00

Ford FI Pickup
1949, 3"
1949 – 1960
(closed tailgate)
$15.00/$20.00/$25.00

Ford FI Pickup
1949, 3"
1949 – 1960
(open tailgate)
$15.00/$20.00/$25.00

Ford FI Pickup
1949, 3"
1949 – 1960
(closed rear window/ribbed bed)
$20.00/$25.00/$30.00

Ford FI Pickup
1949, 3"
1949 – 1960
(Type 2)
$10.00/$15.00/$20.00

Ford Oil Tanker
Texaco, 1949, 6"
1949 – 1952
$35.00/$45.00/$55.00

Ford Oil Tanker
Shell, 1949, 6"
1949 – 1952
$35.00/$45.00/$55.00
Sinclair and Standard brands:
$45.00/$55.00/$65.00

Ford F6, 1949, 4"
1950 – 1969
$15.00/$20.00/$25.00

Ford F6, 1949, 4"
1950 – 1969
(open wheel wells)
$10.00/$15.00/$20.00

Ford F6 Oil
1949, 4"
1950 – 1969
$15.00/$20.00/$25.00

Ford F6 Oil
1949, 4"
(axles inside fenders)
1950 – 1969
$10.00/$15.00/$20.00

Ford Styleside Pickup
1957, 3"
1959 – 1964, 1968 – 1969
(open and closed rear window)
$15.00/$20.00/$25.00

Ford F700 Stake Truck
1956, 6"
1960 – 1964
$20.00/$25.00/$30.00

Ford F700 Stake
1956, 6"
1960 – 1964
Without tin cap top:
$30.00/$40.00/$50.00
With tin cap top:
$60.00/$80.00/$100.00
rare

International KI
Panel, 4"
1947 – 1949
$25.00/$35.00/$45.00

International KI
Panel, 4"
Ambulance
1947 – 1949
(rare)
$35.00/$45.00/$55.00

International KII Oil
Sinclair, 6"
1949 – 1955
$35.00/$45.00/$55.00

International KII
Oil, Standard, 6"
1949 – 1955
$35.00/$45.00/$55.00
Shell & Texaco (very rare):
$45.00/$55.00/$65.00

International Metro Van, 6"
very rare, 1959 only
$100.00/$125.00/$150.00

International K5
Stake, 1947, 6"
(open sides)
1947 – 1953
$30.00/$35.00/$40.00

International K5 Stake
1947, 6"
(closed sides)
1953
Note: with and without ribbed bed
$30.00/$45.00/$55.00

International Car Transport
1947 – 1954
Note: yellow and orange trailers
$35.00/$45.00/$55.00

International Car Transport
1955 – 1958
Note: oval openings trailer
$35.00/$45.00/$55.00

International K5
Gooseneck Trailer, 1947
1949 – 1958
$30.00/$40.00/$50.00

International K5
Grain Hauler, 1947
1949 – 1958
$30.00/$40.00/$50.00

International K5
TOOTSIETOY Semi
1949 – 1958
$35.00/$45.00/$55.00

Mack L-Line Van
Trailer, 1954 – 1959
Note: many decal applications
$90.00/$100.00/$120.00

Mack L-Line Van
TOOTSIETOY Trailer
1954 – 1959
$65.00/$75.00/$85.00

Mack L-Line Oil Tanker
1954 – 1959
Note: ladder rear of trailer
$50.00/$60.00/$70.00

Mack L-Line Log Truck
1955 – 1959
1961, 1963 – 1965
$55.00/$65.00/$75.00

Mack L-Line Machinery Hauler
1947, 1956 – 1960
$55.00/$65.00/$75.00

Mack L-Line
Stakeside Trailer, 1947
1954 – 1959
$85.00/$100.00/$115.00

179

Mack L-Line TOOTSIETOY
Oil Tanker
1954 – 1959
Note: has silver and orange
trailers with decal
$70.00/$80.00/$90.00

Mack L-Line TOOTSIETOY
Line Van Trailer
1954 – 1959
$75.00/$85.00/$95.00

Mack L-Line Hook and Ladder
1956 – 1961
1963 – 1967
$65.00/$75.00/$85.00

Mack L-Line with its
TOOTSIETOY Tin Cap on
1958 – 1959
$50.00/$75.00/$100.00

Mack B-Line Cement Truck
1955, 6"
1959 – 1969
Note: early version had worm axle
to rotate barrel when toy moved
$30.00/$40.00/$50.00

Mack B-Line Utility Trailer
1955, 9"
1960 – 1963
$35.00/$45.00/$55.00

Mack L-Line Semi &
Stake Trailer
1960 – 1963
$90.00/$100.00/$110.00

Mack L-Line Step
Sided Stake
1954 – 1957
$35.00/$40.00/$45.00

Mack L-Line Stake
even sided
1958 – 1959
$40.00/$45.00/$50.00

Mack B-Line Log Truck
1955, 9"
1960, 1967
$55.00/$65.00/$75.00

Mack B-Line Oil
Mobil Tanker, 1955
1960 – 1965, 1967 – 1969
$50.00/$60.00/$70.00

Mack B-Line Oil
Tootsietoy Tanker
1960 – 1967
$65.00/$75.00/$85.00

Note: Other Mack B-Lines are Transport, Boat Transport, Fire Ladder, Machinery, and Pipe. $70.00 – $85.00 each.

RC 180 Machinery
Hauler, 1963 – 1966
$40.00/$50.00/$60.00

RC 180 Oil Tanker
1962
$35.00/$45.00/$55.00

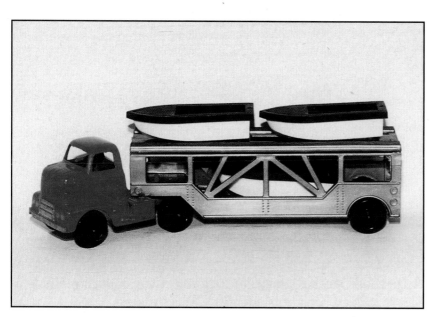

RC 180 Boat Transport
with three boats
1962 – 1967
$65.00/$75.00/$85.00

RC 180 Auto Transport
plastic trailer
1962 – 1964
1968
$50.00/$60.00/$70.00

RC 180 Dean Van Lines
plastic trailer
1963 – 1964
1967
$70.00/$85.00/$100.00

Chevrolet Semi Cab
1959, 1965 – 1966
Note: rare with or without trailer
$80.00/$100.00/$120.00

Came as Auto Transport, Log, Ladder, Oil, Van.

RC 180 Transport
Tin ramp, dual axle trailer
1959 – 1961
$140.00

RC 180 Transport
Tin ramp, single axle trailer
1959 – 1961
$130.00

RC 180 Transport
last version made without tin
ramp and silver trim cab
1959 – 1961?
$100.00

No. 1040 Hook and Ladder (postwar), 4", 1942, 1946, 1948
$65.00/$75.00/$85.00

No. 1041 Hose Car (postwar), 4", 1948 only
$65.00/$75.00/$85.00

No. 104 Insurance Patrol, No. 105 Oil Tanker
1932 – 1934
$25.00/$35.00/$45.00

No. 108 Caterpillar Tractor, No. 109 Stake Truck
1932 – 1934
$25.00/$35.00/$45.00

SEVENTIES TOOTSIETOYS
1970 – 1979

During the 1970s Strombecker Corporation carried several of its later 1960s toys with the new toys of the 1970s. Different color schemes, packaging, and some decal changes were the most obvious changes to their vehicle line up. Every year Strombecker added many new single toys that were sold separately and placed into the various boxed sets.

The Strombecker Corporation had many Tootsietoy midgets that were sold in bulk for the dealers. They were assorted models of unbreakable die-cast metal cars and trucks with steel axles and roll-easy wheels. The toys were roughly 2½" in length and painted in all the popular colors — red, yellow, light blue, dark blue, silver, green, orange, and the light and dark purples. The tiny midgets were placed in many different series and boxed sets. The Collector Series sets usually had a car or truck pulling a small metal trailer with a plastic yacht. A small metal trailer containing a small plastic motorcycle and others were used to make this series somewhat special. The tiny Midgets were also packaged in Jam Pacs™ and placed into Activity sets; No. 1750 Activity Garage, No. 1780 Exclusive Tootsietoy Service Station with its own carrying case. We can't forget the popular No. 1249 Little Toughs truck and trailer assortments. Many models have trailer hooks to pull the many styled trailers. These were easily broken off by being mishandled. I will try to show you all of the Midgets and their packaging in this chapter and in the following pages. These are the most common toys to be found at garage sales and flea markets. Toys still in their original packaging or boxed sets are really rare to stumble onto, but like all other toys the fun is in the search.

Two new assortments were added to the terrific Strombecker line in 1970. They were the No. 1290 Assortment consisting of six trucks and Jeepsters in two body styles. The No. 1295 Assortment also had six different vehicles. This assortment contained a VW, school bus, resort bus, Ford Bronco, dune buggy with surf boards, and an Attex all terrain vehicle. Tootsietoy TOUGHS™ die-cast cars and trucks with realistic detail; bumpers, seats, and chassis. The overall length was 4" for these toys. Tires for these toys were polypropylene wheels with white plastic centered hubs.

These pieces with different paint schemes and decals or stickers were placed in many of the gift sets

and packaged separately. Sets like the No. 1747 Fire Fighters and No. 1840 "Road Master" set just to mention two. The No. 1745 Hitch-Up™ sets were made up of many vehicles pulling trailers with all sorts of boats, motorcycles, and sport vehicles. The first Hitch-Up series™ had eight different 4" vehicles pulling different Tootsietoy accessories. The No. 2535 Tootsietoy Farm Tractor and Spreader was added to this popular line in 1970 as a new item.

The tractor with spreader is the hardest piece to come by and the Ford Bronco by far is the easiest to obtain for your collection.

Tootsietoy Road Haulers consisted of eight different trucks ranging in length from 6½" to 8¼" depending on the trailer length. The same tractor or semi cab was used for the Log Truck, Auto Transport, and the Horse Trailer. The No. 2545 Hook and Ladder is the most common piece in this series of vehicles to locate for your collection. Beware, the fire truck will not always have all its white plastic ladders.

The hardest vehicle in the Road Hauler series of vehicles to find is No. 1930 Tootsietoy, "Double Bottom Dumper." The set had a small HO scale cab pulling to dumper trailers. This is a prime example of a toy carried into the 1970s by Strombecker Corporation. It appeared only in the 1971 and 1972 toy catalogs.

Tootsietoy® Playmates, "Big Slicks," Hop'd Rods, Super Slicks™, Freakies, and many more sets and series were offered in Strombecker catalogs. Road racing sets, cap guns, rifles, pistols, and many of the all plastic vehicles were offered between 1970 and 1979.

Examples of almost all Tootsietoy vehicles and some packaged toys and sets will now grace the following pages. In my opinion, the Collector Series with its HO scaled trucks with trailers, the different hydraulic cranes, as well as the colorful Playmate sets, will be good sets of toys to collect and put into your collection.

For this chapter of my book, I have collected as many examples as possible. However, for the pieces I have not been able to purchase for my collection, I used a few Strombecker color catalog pages.

Happy Collecting!

Pumper, Jeep Truck, 40 Ford, Panel Truck
1970 – 1977
$1.00/$1.50/$2.00

El Camino, MG, Hot Rod, T-Bird
1970 – 1977
$1.00/$1.50/$2.00

Shuttle Truck, Ford J Tow Truck, Oil Truck
1970 – 1977
$1.00/$1.50/$2.00

Volkswagon, Jeep, D-Jaguar, Mustang
1970 – 1977
$1.00/$1.50/$2.00

Porche, Earth Mover, Cadillac, Cheetah
1970 – 1977
$1.00/$1.50/$2.00

Jeepster P-up, Mercedes, Corvette, Formula I
1970 – 1977
$1.00/$1.50/$2.00

West German McDonnell F4C "PHANTOM II"
1970 – 1977
$3.00/$4.00/$5.00

French Dassault IIC "MIRAGE"
1970 – 1977
$3.00/$4.00/$5.00

U. S. Northrop F5A
"LITTLE TIGER"
1970 – 1975
$3.00/$4.00/$5.00

Swedish Saab J35
"DRAGON"
1970 – 1975
$3.00/$4.00/$5.00

Shell Oil Truck
1970 – 1979
$4.00/$6.00/$8.00

"JUMPIN JEEPER"
Jeespter
1970 – 1979
$2.00/$4.00/$6.00

Pumper Fire Truck
1970 – 1979
$3.00/$4.00/$5.00

"WILD WAGON"
1970 – 1979
$2.00/$3.00/$4.00

"WHEELIE WAGON"
1970 – 1979
$2.00/$3.00/$4.00

Jeep
1970 – 1979
$2.00/$3.00/$4.00

1295 CAR ASSORTMENT

"STINGIN BUG" VW
1970 – 1979
$4.00/$6.00/$8.00

"BUZY BEE" School Bus
1970 – 1979
$4.00/$6.00/$8.00

"BIMINI BUGGY" Resort Bus
1970 – 1979
$2.00/$4.00/$6.00

197

"BUCKIN BRONCO" Ford
1970 – 1979
$2.00/$4.00/$6.00

"DUNE BUGGY"
1970 – 1979
$4.00/$6.00/$8.00

ATTEX All Terrain Vehicle
1970 – 1979
$2.00/$4.00/$6.00

1438 (1970) 1249 LITTLE TOUGHS
(1971 – 1979)

Semi-Truck with cab
1970 – 1979
$6.00/$8.00/$10.00

Logger with cab
1970 – 1979
$6.00/$8.00/$10.00

Mobil Gas Tanker
1970
$10.00/$15.00/$20.00

American La France
Fire Engine
1970 – 1979
$4.00/$6.00/$8.00

Aerial Ladder Fire
1970
$8.00/$10.00/$12.00

Dump Truck
1970
$8.00/$10.00/$12.00

Cement Truck
1970
$8.00/$10.00/$12.00

Jeep with Racer, Trailer
1970 – 1979
$6.00/$8.00/$10.00

El Camino with Boat, Trailer
1970 – 1979
$6.00/$8.00/$10.00

1451 Farm Tractor with
Utility Wagon
1970
$15.00/$20.00/$25.00

1452 Heavy Duty
Hydraulic Crane
1970
$15.00/$20.00/$25.00

1456 Honda Motorcycle
with trailer & truck
1970
$8.00/$10.00/$12.00

1460 Auto Transport
1970 – 1979
$15.00/$20.00/$25.00

1468 Car and Cabin Cruizer
1970 – 1979
$8.00/$10.00/$12.00

1469 Truck and Horse Trailer
1970
$25.00/$30.00/$35.00

2522 K-9 Hitch-up
1970 – 1971
$10.00/$15.00/$20.00
NOTE: Eight dogs and clear dome missing.

2523 Honda Hitch-up
1970 – 1975
$6.00/$8.00/$10.00

2524 Cabin Cruizer Hitch-up
1970 – 1976
$8.00/$10.00/$12.00

2525 U-Haul Hitch-up
1970 – 1976
$6.00/$8.00/$10.00

2527 Beach Buggy Hitch-up
1970 – 1975
$6.00/$8.00/$10.00

2528 Snowmobile Hitch-up
1970 – 1975
$10.00/$12.00/$14.00

2529 ATTEX® Hitch-up
1970 – 1976
$10.00/$12.00/$14.00

2535 Farm Tractor and Spreader
1970 – 1973
$15.00/$20.00/$25.00

2831 BLISTER CARDED "JAM PAC"™. New blister carded Jam Pac cars and trucks on a bright illustrated card. 8 die-cast cars packed under a clear, case style, blister. Size 4½" x 12½" packed in shelf display box, (see page 12) 3 dozen to display carton, weight 18 lbs.

2834 TOOTSIETOY "JAM PAC"™ FLEET". "Jam Pac Fleet" is displayed in a 3¾" x 14" frame view box with a formed plastic tray to show the product to its best advantage. Each fleet includes 8 die-cast metal cars and trucks and a set of 3 gas pumps on an island. Pumps have flexible hoses and storage hooks for nozzles. 1 dz. to master carton, weight 6 lbs.

2835 TOOTSIETOY "JAM-PAC"™. 10 top selling die-cast metal miniature cars and trucks. Each is realistically scaled to produce fine detail. Brightly colored assortment is packed in a new, all visual, frame view package. 1 dz. "JAM-PAC"™ to master carton, weight 6 lbs.

jam pac™

NEW

NEW

2835

2831

2834

die cast planes & trains

2850 JET FIGHTERS. 3 die-cast replicas of popular fighter jets with colorful authentic wing markings. Models include Swedish Saab J 35 "Dragon," U. S. Northrop F 5A "Little Tiger," West German McDonnell F4C "Phantom" and French Dassault IIIC "Mirage." 1 dz. to carton, weight 5 lbs.

2855 TRAIN. 6-piece, highly detailed, train measures 16" overall. Hitches together easily for pull-along play. Cars include diesel engine, coal car, reefer, covered hopper, cattle car and caboose. 1 dz. to carton, weight 6½ lbs.

2850 JET FIGHTERS.

2855 TRAIN.

1971 catalog page showing JAM PAC™, Die-cast planes & trains
2831 Blister carded – $18.00
2834 Tootsie Fleet – $20.00
2835 Tootsie carded – $22.00
2850 Jet Fighters – $20.00
2855 Train (6 piece) – $25.00

2940 Dump Truck, 6¼"
1970 – 1979
$9.00/$12.00/$15.00

2941 Sanitation Truck, 6½"
1970 – 1979
$9.00/$12.00/$15.00

2543 Cement Truck, 6"
1970 – 1979
$9.00/$12.00/$15.00

2545 Hook & Ladder, 7¼"
1970 – 1974
$9.00/$12.00/$15.00

2550 Logger, 7½"
1970 – 1975
$12.00/$15.00/$18.00

2555 Horse Trailer, 8¼"
1970 – 1975
$10.00/$15.00/$20.00

2920 Auto Transport, 8½"
1970 – 1975
$9.00/$12.00/$15.00

1930 "Double Bottom Dumper" (Rare)
1970, 1971
$15.00/$20.00/$25.00

TOOTSIETOY PLAYMATES

2024 TOMMY TRACTOR 6½"
1970 – 1972
$10.00/$15.00/$20.00

2025 PETER PILOT, 7"
1970 – 1972
$10.00/$15.00/$20.00

2026 RONNIE RACER 6½"
1970 – 1972
$10.00/$15.00/$20.00

TOOTSIETOY®
super slicks™

2944 SUPER SLICKS™. Six assorted "wayout" custom style fun cars. Features include "Sculptured Look" die-cast metal bodies, beautiful show color paint, super wide slick racing tires, chrome plated wheels and engines, interior detail, steering wheel, decals and windshields. Assortment includes Pie Wagon, Twin Shaft, Dune Buster, Desert Fox, Bandito, and Panzer Wagon. Size of cars 4¼". All Blister packed on crazy color cards. 1 dozen to carton. Weight 4 lbs.

DUNE BUSTER

DESERT FOX

PANZER WAGON

TWIN SHAFT

BANDITO

PIE WAGON

Catalog page showing SUPER SLICKS ™
1971 – 1976
$3.00/$5.00/$7.00

2950 FREAKIES

"SWEAT-T"
1971 – 1973
$10.00/$15.00/$20.00

"DRAGON DRAGSTER"
1971 – 1973
$10.00/$15.00/$20.00

"TIJUANA TARANTULA"
1971 – 1973
$10.00/$15.00/$20.00

MICKEY MILK
1971
$25.00

FARMER JONES
1971
$25.00

HOKY SMOKY
1971
$25.00

activity sets

1750 ACTIVITY GARAGE. A modern automatic Super Service Station with action features. Car wash section has turntable, push rod, and crank. Tihs assembly moves the car through 3 sponge wash rollers. When car has been washed it will roll down ramp through "CRASH CORNER" intersection. Station has a fast car start lane with spring loaded push button release. Elevating grease ramp for car lubrication. Service station building has side windows and skylights. 6 gasoline pumps with moveable hoses. 4 die-cast metal cars and trucks complete the fun. Size 2$\frac{1}{2}$x8x11. 6 each to carton, weight 4 lbs.

1751 SUPER AIRPORT. The world's busiest airport all in one package. ACTION, ACTION, ACTION. Airport control panel activates the set. Right hand throttle handle raises inspection ramp inside of hanger for engine inspection; reverse handle and plane will roll down ramp. Push left hand throttle and airplane will turn 180° on vector selector turntable until operator selects runway direction desired. Turn the roll out control and aircraft will slowly move out onto the field. Load plane catapult and push release button for fast take-off. Brightly colored and checker-board decorated. Hanger comes complete with 3 die-cast metal airplanes, Size 3$\frac{1}{2}$x8x11. 6 each to carton, weight 4 lbs.

1780 EXCLUSIVE TOOTSIETOY SERVICE STATION CARRYING CASE. Unique service station folds up into easily transported carrying case. Station is made of high-impact plastic with pull-out car ramp. Cars may travel up the ramp to second floor parking area. Garage doors lift up and down. Case opens to form a generous service area complete with 10 Tootsietoy cars, illustrated gas pumps, oil racks, and roadways. Carrying handle on side of case. Size 2$\frac{1}{2}$"x5"x12". Packed 12 each to master carton, weight 26 lbs.

CASE SHOWN OPEN

CASE FOLDS INTO COMPACT CARRYING CASE

COMPLETE WITH 10 CARS

9

1970 catalog page, ACTIVITY SETS
1970 – 1971
1750 Activity Garage – $35.00
1751 Super Airport – $35.00
1780 Service Station – $40.00

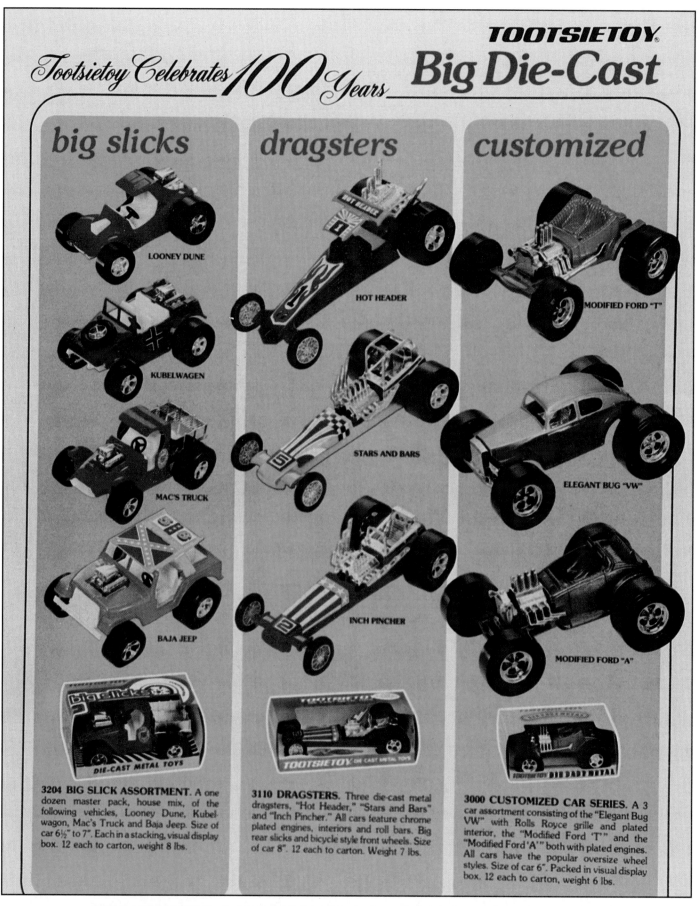

Tootsietoy Celebrates 100 Years

TOOTSIETOY Big Die-Cast

big slicks

LOONEY DUNE

KUBELWAGEN

MAC'S TRUCK

BAJA JEEP

3204 BIG SLICK ASSORTMENT. A one dozen master pack, house mix, of the following vehicles, Looney Dune, Kubelwagon, Mac's Truck and Baja Jeep. Size of car 6½" to 7". Each in a stacking, visual display box. 12 each to carton, weight 8 lbs.

dragsters

HOT HEADER

STARS AND BARS

INCH PINCHER

3110 DRAGSTERS. Three die-cast metal dragsters, "Hot Header," "Stars and Bars" and "Inch Pincher." All cars feature chrome plated engines, interiors and roll bars. Big rear slicks and bicycle style front wheels. Size of car 8". 12 each to carton. Weight 7 lbs.

customized

MODIFIED FORD "T"

ELEGANT BUG "VW"

MODIFIED FORD "A"

3000 CUSTOMIZED CAR SERIES. A 3 car assortment consisting of the "Elegant Bug VW" with Rolls Royce grille and plated interior, the "Modified Ford 'T'" and the "Modified Ford 'A'" both with plated engines. All cars have the popular oversize wheel styles. Size of car 6". Packed in visual display box. 12 each to carton, weight 6 lbs.

3400 BIG SLICKS, 3100 DRAGSTERS 1972 – 1976, CUSTOMIZED 1974 – 1976
3204 each $3.00/$5.00/$7.00 – 3110 each $6.00/$8.00/$10.00 – 3000 each $3.00/$5.00/$7.00

1972 catalog page showing HOP'D RODS, 1972 – 1976
No. 2400
$2.00/$4.00/$6.00

new!

KOOL KARS

1240 KOOL KARS. 3 assorted custom racing cars with big wheels, and the real Kool "Raked Look." Die-cast metal bodies, silver painted interiors and engines. Assortment includes the Sand "Flee," "Screecher Creature," and Drag "Asp." Size of cars 2¾". Blister packed on racy style cards. 3 dozen to carton. Weight 7 lbs. Prepriced 49¢.

SAND FLEE

DRAG ASP

SCREECHER CREATURE

1972 catalog photo KOOL KARS, 1972 – 1975
No. 1240
$2.00/$4.00/$6.00

U.S. M-8 Armored Car
1973 – 1976
$5.00/$7.00/$9.00

British Mark II Armored Car
1973 – 1976
$5.00/$7.00/$9.00

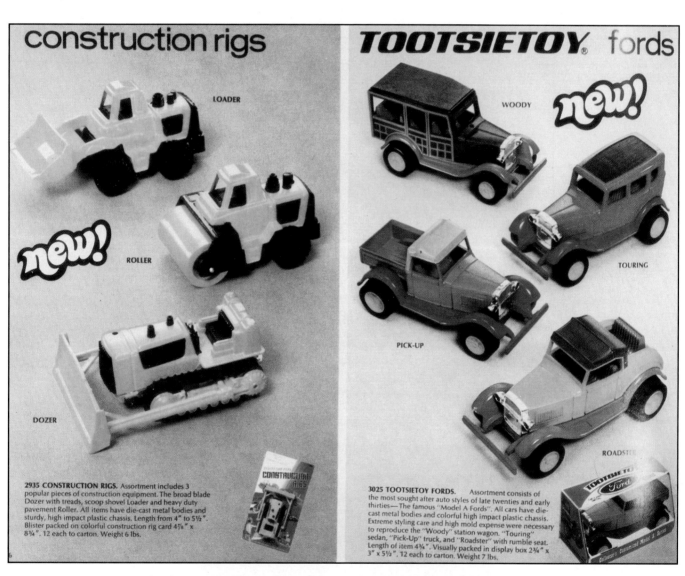

construction rigs

LOADER

ROLLER

new!

DOZER

2935 CONSTRUCTION RIGS. Assortment includes 3 popular pieces of construction equipment. The broad blade Dozer with treads, scoop shovel Loader and heavy duty pavement Roller. All items have die-cast metal bodies and sturdy, high impact plastic chassis. Length from 4" to 5½". Blister packed on colorful construction rig card 4⅞" x 8¼". 12 each to carton. Weight 6 lbs.

TOOTSIETOY® fords

WOODY

new!

TOURING

PICK-UP

ROADSTER

3025 TOOTSIETOY FORDS. Assortment consists of the most sought after auto styles of late twenties and early thirties— The famous "Model A Fords". All cars have die-cast metal bodies and colorful high impact plastic chassis. Extreme styling care and high mold expense were necessary to reproduce the "Woody" station wagon. "Touring" sedan, "Pick-Up" truck, and "Roadster" with rumble seat. Length of item 4¾". Visually packed in display box 2¾" x 3" x 5½". 12 each to carton. Weight 7 lbs.

2935 CONSTRUCTION RIGS & 3025 TOOTSIETOY FORDS
2935 – $2.00/$3.00/$4.00 (each)
3025 – $5.00/$10.00/$15.00 (each)

1296 ARMY TOUGHS

Deuce ½ Truck
1973 – 1976
$2.00/$4.00/$6.00

U.S. Jeep
1973 – 1976
$2.00/$4.00/$6.00

German Kubelwagon
1973 – 1976
$2.00/$4.00/$6.00

105 MM Howitzer
1973 – 1976
$1.00/$1.50/$2.00

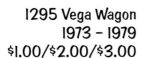

1295 Vega Wagon
1973 – 1979
$1.00/$2.00/$3.00

1295 Gremlin
1973 – 1979
$2.00/$3.00/$4.00

HITCH-UP™ SERIES

2524 Speed Boat
1970 – 1976
$6.00/$8.00/$10.00

2530 Kubelwagon and Cannon
1973 – 1975
$6.00/$8.00/$10.00

2537 Deuce ½
Military truck and trailer
1973 – 1975
$6.00/$8.00/$10.00

2538 Airstream trailer and Vega car
1973 – 1975
$6.00/$8.00/$10.00

2539 ATC Honda cycle & Gremlin car
1973 – 1975
$6.00/$8.00/$10.00

2435 Farm Tractor
1974 – 1977
$8.00/$10.00/$12.00

2544 Camper
1974 – 1976
$8.00/$10.00/$12.00

2548
School Bus
1974 – 1977
$6.00/$8.00/$10.00

Ferrari #8
1974 – 1977
$2.00/$4.00/$6.00

Porche #4
1974 – 1977
$2.00/$4.00/$6.00

Can Am
1974 – 1977
$2.00/$4.00/$6.00

IOII MIDGETS ADDED TO 1974

Fiat Abarth, Custom Rod, Tornado, and Dragster
1974 – 1977
$1.00/$1.50/$2.00

Roadster, Run-A-Bout, Land Rover
1974 – 1977
$1.00/$1.50/$2.00

Durant® plastic car series

new!

new!

THE THING (VW)

'34 FORD "VICKY"

DESERT DEVIL

BANANA PEELER

ROD N' RAIL

5050 "VW"-"VICKY" ASST. 12 each assorted of the following 2 cars. Weight 6 lbs.

5050 THE THING. VW latest entry in the auto world. Combines the rustic features of an "off the road" vehicle with the advantages of a standard sedan. Bright plated front and rear lights. Rag top style roof, chassis pan, big wheels combined with large scale of item, give the car the "BIG" look. Overall length 11½". 12 each, bulk packed to carton. Weight 6 lbs.

5050 34 FORD VICTORIA "5 WINDOW COUPE". The most popular auto style for '34 was the "5 window VICKY." Reproduced with all its flowing curves and graceful front plated grill. Due to its scale this coupe has the "BIG" look for plastic cars. Overall length 11½". 12 each, bulk packed to carton. Weight 6 lbs.

5011 "FUNNY CAR" ASST. 12 each assorted of the following 3 cars. Weight 6 lbs.

5011 DESERT DEVIL RECONNAISSANCE CAR. California Baja Desert fun car. A civilian revamp style of the great Mercedes military car of past fame. Extra wheels for sand traction. Lots of chrome details, wheels, radiator lights, windshield frame, rear tire cover. Overall length 11". 12 each, bulk packed to carton. Weight 6 lbs.

5011 BANANA PEELER DRAGSTER. Latest dragster with enclosed driver's seat and custom styled rear end. Plated engine, twin plated fuel tanks, sculptural body design, huge rear slicks with plated wheels, bicycle front tires with plated spokes. Overall length 12". 12 each, bulk packed to carton. Weight 6 lbs.

5011 ROD N' RAIL, EXTENDED HOT ROD. "C" cab custom style body with extended frame, make a mighty slick look for any drag track. Plated engine with chrome fuel tanks, coach lamps, and chute. Huge rear racing slicks with chrome wheels and bicycle front drag tires with chrome spokes. Overall length 10". 12 each, bulk packed to carton. Weight 6 lbs.

5025 PLASTIC CAR DISPLAY. 36 each cars packed into a shipper, shelf display.

13

1974 catalog page DURANT® PLASTIC CAR SERIES
$2.00/$3.00/$4.00

1297 RESCUE VEHICLES

Personnel Truck
1975 – 1979
$1.00/$2.00/$3.00

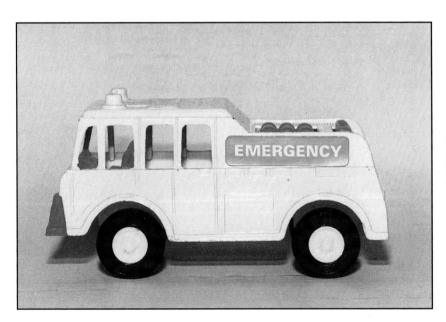

Equipment Truck
1975 – 1979
$1.00/$2.00/$3.00

Paramedic Ambulance
1975 – 1979
$1.50/$2.50/$3.50

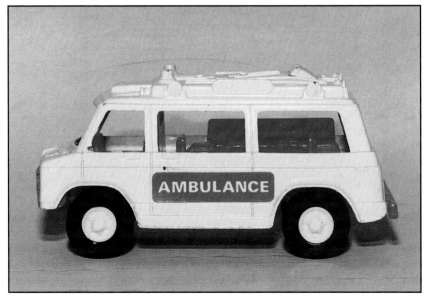

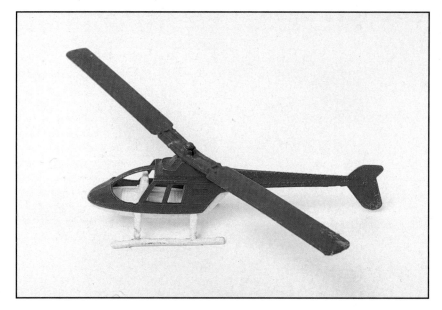

2552 Rescue Helicopter
1975 – 1979
$6.00/$8.00/$10.00

1295 Dune Buggy
1975 – 1979
$2.00/$3.00/$4.00

2527 Beach Buggy
Hitch-up™
1970 – 1975
$6.00/$8.00/$10.00

1250 TOOTSIETOY TINY TOUGHS

Van
1975 – 1979
$1.00/$3.00/$5.00

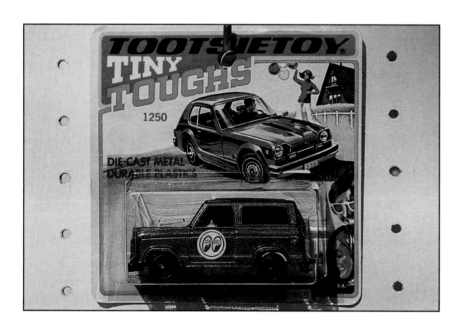

Chevy Blazer
1975 – 1979
$1.00/$3.00/$5.00

Honda Civic
1975 – 1979
$1.00/$3.00/$5.00

VW Bug
1975 – 1979
$2.00/$4.00/$6.00

Land Rover
1975 – 1979
$1.00/$3.00/$5.00

Pickup
1975 – 1979
$2.00/$4.00/$6.00

Motorcycle and trailer pulled by Van
1976 – 1979
$4.00/$6.00/$8.00

VW pulling house trailer
1976 – 1979
$4.00/$6.00/$8.00

2302 TINY TOUGHS SEMIS

Gravel
1976 – 1979
$6.00/$8.00/$10.00

Semi Trailer
1976 – 1979
$7.00/$9.00/$11.00

Logger
1976 – 1979
$7.00/$9.00/$11.00

2303 TINY TOUGHS
HIGHWAY VEHICLES

Greyhound Bus, 5"
1976 – 1979
$6.00/$8.00/$10.00

Fire Truck with ladder, 5"
1976 – 1979
$6.00/$8.00/$10.00

Camper with mural
1976 – 1979
$8.00/$10.00/$12.00

1299 TOOTSIETOY S.W.A.T. TRUCKS

Police Van
1976 – 1979
$2.00/$3.00/$4.00

Armored Car
1976 – 1979
$4.00/$6.00/$8.00

Special Equipment Truck
1976 – 1979
$3.00/$5.00/$7.00

2200 Sports Van
1977 – 1979
$3.00/$5.00/$7.00

2980 F-16 plane
1977 – 1979
$8.00/$10.00/$12.00

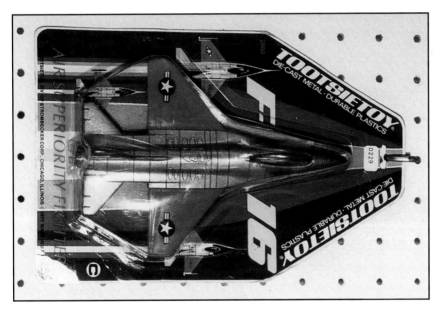

2216 Adventure
Exploring vehicle unit
1977
$1.00/$3.00/$5.00

2220 Scorpion Helicopter
1977 – 1979
$4.00/$6.00/$8.00

2210 SPECIAL MISSION VEHICLES

Custom Van
1977 – 1978
$1.00/$2.00/$3.00

Off-Road Pickup
1977 – 1979
$1.00/$2.00/$3.00

Special Equipment Truck
1977 – 1978
$1.00/$2.00/$3.00

Forward Cab Truck
1977 – 1978
$1.00/$2.00/$3.00

Special Speed Racer
1977 – 1978
$1.50/$2.50/$3.50

239

3260 Tootsietoy
Red Baron
tri-plane
1978 – 1979
$10.00/$15.00/$20.00

"WIDE-BODY" SERIES

3152
Fire Truck with a ladder
1978 – 1979
$2.00/$3.00/$4.00

3160 Sport Van with canoe
1977 – 1978
$2.50/$3.50/$4.50

2975 TOOTSIETOY WAR SHIPS

Battleship
1978 – 1979
$2.00/$4.00/$6.00

Aircraft Carrier
1978 – 1979
$3.00/$5.00/$7.00

2080 TOOTSIETOY SEA POWER

Destroyer
1978 – 1979
$2.00/$4.00/$6.00

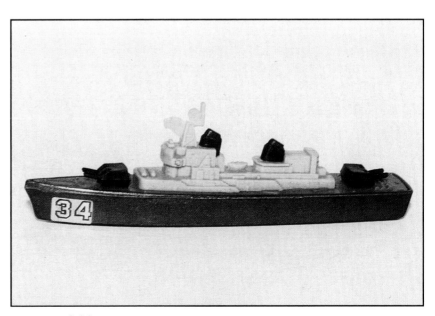

Submarine
1978 – 1979
$2.00/$4.00/$6.00

Cargo Ship
1978 – 1979
$2.00/$4.00/$6.00

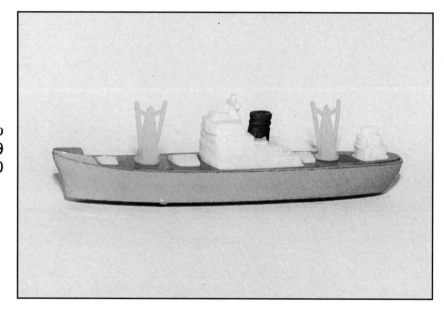

2406 Tootsietoy Tow Truck
1978 – 1979
$3.00/$5.00/$7.00

2990 KEEP ON TRUCKING

Pepsi Truck Semi
1979
$6.00/$8.00/$10.00

RC Truck Semi
1979
$6.00/$8.00/$10.00

CB Truck Semi
1979
$6.00/$8.00/$10.00

2873 Dirt Track
Racing Bike
1979
$4.00/$5.00/$6.00

3140 Rover 4 x 4
1978 – 1979
$2.00/$3.00/$4.00

3140 Subaru Brat
1978 – 1979
$2.00/$3.00/$4.00

3180 Tootsietoy
Dump Truck
1979
$4.00/$6.00/$8.00

3185 Tootsietoy
F4U Corsair
1979
$6.00/$8.00/$10.00

3210 Catering Truck
1979
$6.00/$8.00/$10.00

3166 Tootsietoy
Sport Airplane
1979
$6.00/$8.00/$10.00

3168 Tootsietoy Blazer
(side boards)
1978 – 1979
$2.00/$3.00/$4.00

3168 Tootsietoy Blazer
(no side boards)
1978 – 1979
$2.00/$3.00/$4.00

3151 Emergency
Rescue Truck
1978 – 1979
$3.00/$5.00/$7.00

3152 Fire Truck
1978 – 1979
$3.00/$5.00/$7.00

3150 TV News Helicopter
1978 – 1979
$3.00/$5.00/$7.00

3205 Tootsietoy
Soft Drink Truck (RC)
1979
$10.00/$15.00/$20.00

3185 Tootsietoy
Air Races
1979
$8.00/$10.00/$12.00

5014 36 Ford
"Cruzin'" Coupe
1979
$2.00/$4.00/$6.00

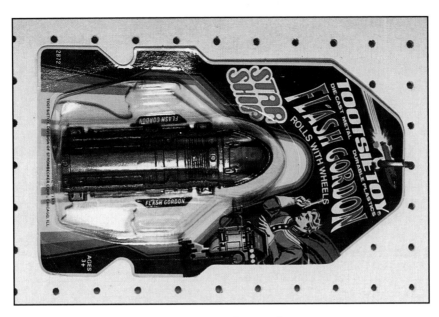

Flash Gordon Space Ship
1978 – 1979
$6.00/$8.00/$10.00

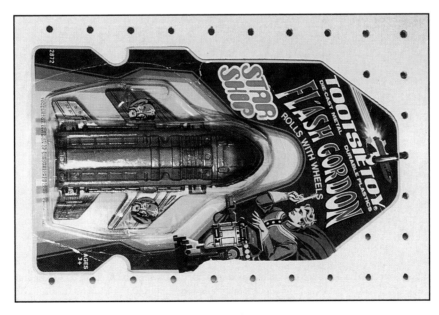

Ming Space Ship
1978 – 1979
$6.00/$8.00/$10.00

TOOTSIETOYS PACKAGED TOYS AND BOXED SETS
1970 – 1979

Tootsietoy had various methods of packaging their brightly painted and decorated toys. The early 1970, No. 1290 and No. 1295 car and truck assortments were packed in a clear, stackable, blister case with a printed roadway base. This was changed in 1971 to a brightly illustrated card. Cars and trucks were packed under a clear, blister case for easy display.

The many boxed sets of toys were often placed in a white plastic tray, bordered by colorful cardboard, and then completely sealed with a plastic or cellophane-type material.

A single toy or boxed set in its original packaging will usually add 15 to 20 percent to the price of the toy or sets. Strombecker produced over 90 different packaged sets between 1970 and 1979. Some are rather scarce today because they were only produced in limited numbers and carried for one or two years in the Strombecker toy catalogs of the 1970s.

The following pages will illustrate some examples of Tootsietoys in their original packaging.

1055 Swedish Jet, 1970
$15.00

1290 Dune Buggy
1970
$16.00

1438 Jeep and Trailer
1970
$18.00

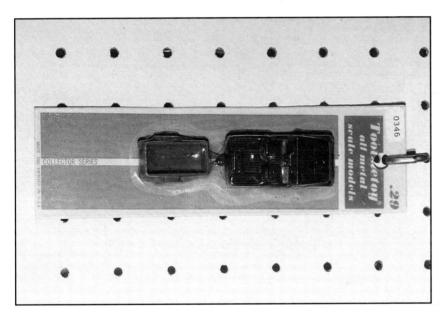

1682 Construction Set
1970
$20.00

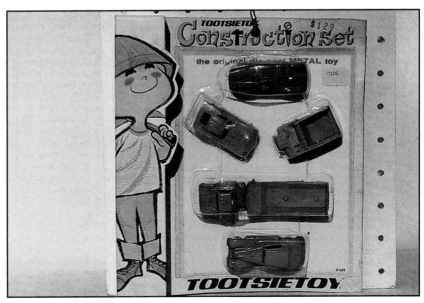

Flatbed with Jaguar
$15.00

Ladder Truck
$15.00

Hydraulic Crane
$25.00

40 Ford, motorcycle, and trailer
$15.00

Dune Buggy, motorcycle, and trailer
$15.00

Jeep, boat, and trailer
$15.00

Dune Buggy, boat, and trailer
$15.00

Log Truck
$15.00

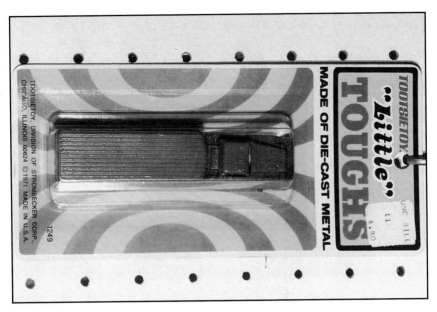

Semi van trailer truck
$18.00

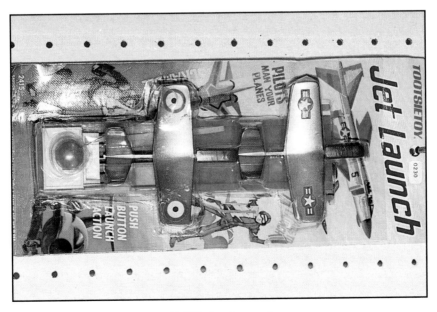

2415 Jet Launch
1972
$15.00

3100 Super Twist
1972
$15.00

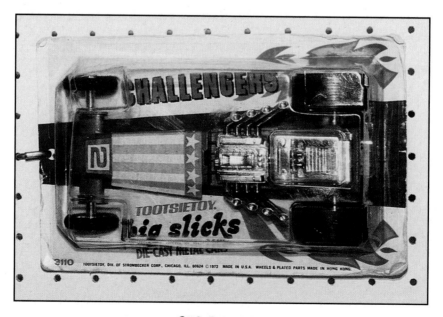

3110 Dragster
1972
$20.00

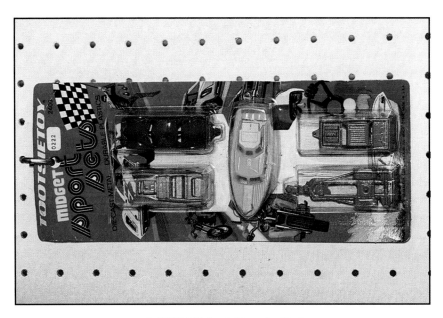

2405 Midget Sports Set
1974
$15.00

2552 Rescue Chopper
$12.00

2220 Scorpion Chopper
1976
$10.00

2080 WAR SHIPS 1978

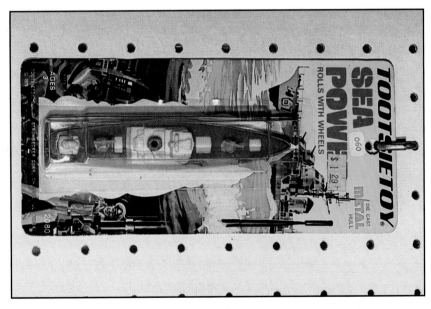

Cargo Ship
$8.00

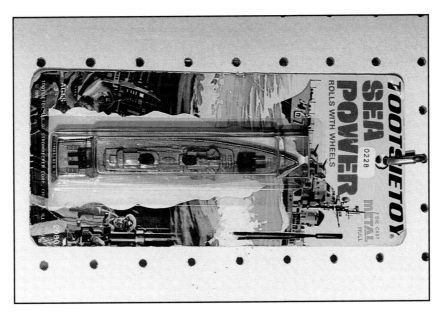

Destroyer Ship
$8.00

Submarine
$8.00

1295 Exxon Oil
1977 – 1979
$8.00

1295 Forestry Truck
1977 – 1979
$8.00

1299 S.W.A.T. Van
1976
$8.00

1732 Spearhead Set
1973
$25.00

1745 Hitch-ups™
1971
$25.00

1760 Sportsters
1971
$40.00

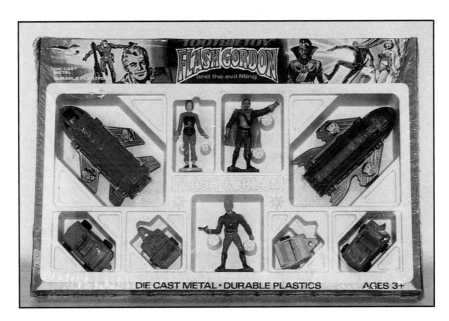

1793 Flash Gordon Set, 1978
$50.00

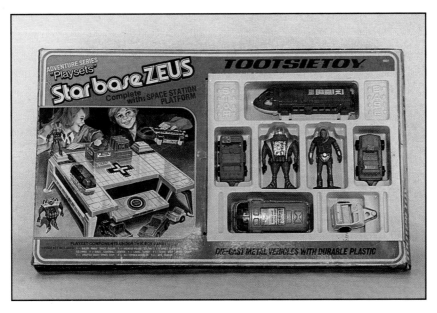

1801 Starbase Zeus, 1977
$60.00

This section consists of all the boxed and packaged sets produced between 1970 – 1979. The number for each set is the actual catalog number taken from original catalogs. You will find the years they were in production beside each set. At this time there are no prices available. However, prices should be between $15.00 and $75.00 depending on the availability of each set.

1640 TOOTSIETOY CONSTRUCTION SET: (1979)
Set contains dump truck, 4 x 4 pickup, and bulldozer, Also included are four small pylons and two road block signs.

1642 TOOTSIETOY EMERGENCY SET: (1979)
Set contains wide body police and fire truck, helicopter, and four action figures.

1654 TOOTSIETOY SPORT SET: (1979)
Set contains sport truck wide body pulling two motorcycles on a trailer. A tough 4 x 4 pulling four canoes on a special trailer.

1665 TOOTSIETOY TOLLWAY SET: (1979)
Set contains two wide body die-cast metal trucks, four highway pylons, and a highly detailed two-station operating toll plaza.

1666 TOOTSIETOY DIRT BIKE SET: (1979)
Set contains two wide body die-cast vehicles, two dirt bikes, dirt bike trailer, and two plastic riders.

1667 TOOTSIETOY CATERING & SOFT DRINK SET: (1979)
Set contains two different wide-body trucks. Catering with two small plastic cases and soft drink truck with two small cases and two small carts.

1686 FARM EQUIPMENT SET: (1970 – 1971)
Set contains a heavy-duty tractor with high rear fenders, four unit disc harrow, double shear plow, and utility wagon.

1689 AIRPORT SET: (1970 – 1972)
Set contains cast metal airplane, gas tanker, landing Jeep, Jeepster car, and Jeep truck.

1690 TRUCK FLEET SET: (1970 – 1972)
Set contains logger, cab and semi-trailer, Jeep truck, three logs, and six barrels.

1691 FIRE FIGHTING SET: (1970 – 1972)
Set contains aerial ladder truck, emergency Jeep, first aid panel truck, pumper, chief's car, and badge.

1692 CONSTRUCTION SET: (1970 – 1972)
Set contains skip loader, earth mover, cab with equipment trailer, Jeep, and low side shuttle truck.

1694 CAR FLEET SET (1970 – 1971)
Set contains six die-cast cars and trucks and boat and trailer.

1704 CROSS COUNTRY SET (1970 – 1972)
Set contains 14 pieces. Nine cars and trucks, midget racer, racer trailer, boat with trailer, and game spinner.

1704 TRAFFIC CONTROL SET (1970 – 1972)
Set contains 11 pieces. Two choppers, police badge, four cars, Honda cycle, transport unit with cab, and game spinner.

1705 CAMPER COMBO SET (1971 – 1973)
Set contains a new "Pop Top" camper hitched to a new Super Clicks™ car.

1711 STARBASE SET: (1977 – 1978)
Set consists of the following: Major Mars space figure, shuttle craft spaceship, all-terrain vehicle, and ATV trailer.

1712 BIO-TRONIC MAN: (1977 – 1978)
Set consists of the following: Bio-Tronic Man figure, Tootsietoy truck, motorcycle, and motorcycle trailer.

1714 CAPT. LAZER:
Set consists of the following: Capt. Lazer hero figure, Tootsietoy car, watercraft with trailer.

1722 TOOTSIETOY TINY TOUGHS CAR SET: (1975 – 1977)
Set contains a camping trailer, fishing boat with trailer, motorcycle with trailer, and two die-cast metal pulling trucks.

1723 TOOTSIETOY RV, RECREATION VEHICLE SET: (1976 – 1977)
Set contains a camping trailer, fishing boat with trailer, motorcycle with trailer, and two die-cast metal pulling trucks.

1724 TOOTSIETOY "KEEP ON TRUCKING" SET: (1976 – 1978)
Set contains semi trailer truck with pulling cab, logger truck, and gravel hauler trailer truck.

1730 GRAND PRIX RACING SET: (1974 – 1975)
Set contains five European race circuit cars. Ferrari, Porsche, Can Am, and two Custom Team Racers.

1731 OPEN ROAD CAMPING SET: (1973 – 1979)
Set contains camping trailer, Vega station wagon, run-a-bout outboard boat, die-cast boat trailer. Also Gremlin car and Suzuki dirt bike.

1732 SPEARHEAD MILITARY SET: (1973 – 1977)
Set contains seven pieces of military items. Kubelwagon

car, 105mm Howitzer cannon, deuce ½ Army truck with missle rest, two LaCross missiles, Army Jeep, and trailer.

1733 TOOTSIETOY CALIFORNIA FUN TIME: (1979)
Set contains hang glider action with two sports figures, custom van, off road pickup truck, fun wagon, and floatable raft.

1736 TOOTSIETOY JET FLIGHT SET: (1979)
Set contains F-16 Jet Fighter serviced for flight by fuel truck, utility truck, crew transport, and support trailer.

1740 TRAVEL SET: (1970 – 1972)
Set contains a six piece hitch together train, two modern jets, six die-cast cars, a speed boat, and three pump gas island.

1741 PLAYTIME SET: (1970 – 1972)
Set contains both aerial ladder and pumper fire trucks, helicopter, construction vehicles, pickup, oil tanker, Jeep, earth mover, shuttle truck, panel truck, Jeepster, tow truck, and four cars.

1742 TOOTSIETOY S.W.A.T. GIFT SET: (1976 – 1977)
Set contains three vehicles, search light, and four S.W.A.T. plastic figures.

1745 HITCH-UP TM SET: (1970 – 1979)
Set contains various vehicles pulling boat, cycle, and other metal vehicles. All years contain different vehicles.

1746 ROADMASTER JR. SET: (1972 – 1979)
Set contains auto transport trailer and modern cab with windows. Three die-cast cars or trucks with two additional cars for transport trailer.

1747 FIRE FIGHTERS SET: (1970 – 1979)
Set contains aerial ladder, die-cast fire truck, chemical truck, pumper truck with two ladders, and chief's badge.

1748 FARM SET: (1970 – 1979)
Set contains farm tractor and spreader cart, horse van trailer unit with six horses, and runabout truck.

1749 TOOTSIETOY EMERGENCY "RESCUE 1" SET: (1975 – 1979)
Set contains four exciting rescue vehicles and the Bell "Jet Ranger" Helicopter.

1750 ACTIVITY GARAGE SET: (1970 – 1971)
Set contains Super Service Station with action carwash, grease ramp, six gas pumps, and four cars or trucks.

1750 TOOTSIETOY "AMERICAN ROAD" SET: (1976 – 1977)
Set contains three die-cast pulling cars, motorcycle with trailer, fishing boat with boat trailer, camping trailer, and a Winnebago RV Vehicle.

1751 SUPER AIRPORT SET: (1970 – 1971)
Set contains three die-cast airplanes, hangar, and action control panel with hand throttle.

1753 CHOPPER SET: (1972 – 1973)
Set contains three latest style hogs. Trikes are "Kraut Chopper," "Black Knight," and "Myster Hogger."

1754 STARBASE BETA SET: (1977 – 1978)
Set consists of the following: Major Mars figure, his enemy the android Zoltan, starship space craft, shuttle craft spaceship, two all-terrain vehicles, and ATV trailer.

1756 CHALLENGER DRAGSTER SET: (1972 – 1973)
Set contains two 8" long dragsters, and "Stars and Bars Special," and the "Inch Pincher."

1758 BIO-TRONIC MAN II SET: (1977 – 1978)
Set consists of the following: Bio-Tronic Man figure, F-16 airplane, Bio-Tronic equipment truck, forward cab pickup truck, and motorcycle with trailer.

1759 CAPT. LAZER AND THE GREAT APE: (1977 – 1978)
Set consists of the following: Capt. Lazer hero figure, his enemy the Great Ape, Capt. Lazer's hero car, custom van truck, pickup truck, watercraft with trailer.

1760 SPORTSTER SET: (1971 – 1979)
Set contains 13 pieces including the Attex, two Honda motorcycles with trailer, dune buggy, boat with trailer, Snow Cat snowmobile, and four rough-going trucks.

1762 TOOTSIETOY FORDS: (1974 – 1976)
Set contains four famous Model A Fords. Extreme stying care and high mold expense went to produce the Woody station wagon, Touring sedan, pickup truck, and Roadster with rumble seats.

1764 TOOTSIETOY TASK FORCE 88 SET: (1978 – 1979)
Set contains battleship, aircraft carrier, destroyer, cargo ship, and submarine.

1765 ARMORED PATROL MILITARY SET: (1973 – 1976)
Set contains two die-cast armored cars, Kubelwagen, 105mm Howitzer cannon, Army truck, Army Jeep, and deuce ½ truck with missle rest and LaCross missle.

1768 THE TOOTSIETOY CONSTRUCTION CO. SET: (1974 – 1976)
Set contains dozer, roller, loader, and three other construction vehicles.

1770 "BIG SLICKS" ATV HITCH UP SET: (1972)
Set contains large die-cast car with large wheels pulling a trailer with an off-the-road vehicle on it.

1772 "BIG SLICKS" TRAIL BIKE HITCH UP SET: (1972 – 1974)
Set contains large die-cast car pulling a trailer containing two Honda #70 Trail Bikes.

1775 "BIG SLICKS" CHOPPER HITCH UP SET: (1972 – 1973)
Set contains large die-cast metal car with three wheel die-cast metal chopper and metal trailer.

1780 EXCLUSIVE TOOTSIETOY SERVICE STATION CARRYING CASE: (1970 – 1971)
Set contains service station that folds out within its own case. A car ramp and 10 cars and trucks. Case has its own handle on side.

1790 TOOTSIETOY "CB" HIGHWAY SET: (1977 – 1979)
Set contains all the latest highway equipment associated with the CB craze. Large express semi-trailer/tractor truck rig, California van, 2-wheeler Honda motorcycle with trailer, Smokey Bear Police car, large camper, police "spy in the sky" helicopter, and CB microphone with push button action.

1792 TOOTSIETOY POLICE SET: (1978 – 1979)
Set contains van, special equipment van, police personnel truck, emergency truck, search light, helicopter, motorcycle, badge, and two road block barricades.

1793 TOOTSIETOY FLASH GORDON C SET: (1978 – 1979)
Set contains popular movie and T.V. heros featured in action space set. Included are "Flash Gordon" starship, "Ming" starship, two surface explorer vehicles with two trailers, Flash Gordon, Ming, and Dale plastic figures.

1800 TOOTSIETOY LARGE S.W.A.T. GIFT SET: (1976 – 1977)
Set contains the complete "Special Weapons and Tactics" team vehicle set, a helicopter, three plastic figures, moveable search light, and five different 4" S.W.A.T. trucks.

1801 STARBASE ZEUS: (1977 – 1978)
Set made of high impact material, quality molded, playset components for space station platform. Set has two figures and five vehicles.

1802 BIO-TRONIC LABORATORY: (1977 – 1978)
Set made of high impact material, quality molded playset components for Bio-Tronic Lab. Complete with Tootsietoy die-cast metal vehicles.

1803 CAPT. LAZER'S SECRET HIDEOUT: (1977 – 1978)
Set made of high impact material, quality molded playset components for secret hideout. Grid system layout for various playset arrangements. Set has two figures and five different vehicles.

1805 TOOTSIETOY FAIR ACRES FARM SET: (1970)
Set contains realistic two-story barn, fenced coral holds two horses, two pigs, two cows, and one chicken. Farm tractor, disc harrow, plow, utility wagon, Jeep truck, pickup truck, overland Jeep and skip loader.

1805 TOOTSIETOY "INTERSTATE" SET: (1976 – 1979)
Set contains the complete highway set. Includes four pulling metal cars, Greyhound bus, semi trailer truck, logger truck, and gravel hauler truck.

1810 TOOTSIETOY FIRE STATION SET: (1970)
Set contains plastic fire station, snorkel truck, pumper, panel truck, fire chief's badge, net, ladders, fire axes, and stretcher.

1815 TOOTSIETOY FIGHTER COMMAND SET: (1979)
Set contains highly detailed WWII Fighter serviced for missions by fuel truck, utility truck, crew transport, and support trailer. Four military figures and transporter guard ground operations.

1830 TOOTSIETOY EMERGENCY "RESCUE 2" SET: (1975 – 1978)
Set contains two Bell "Jet Ranger" rescue helicopters, paramedic ambulance, equipment truck, personnel truck, aerial ladder truck, and three other popular service trucks.

1835 TOOTSIETOY FLYING PATROL: (1979)
Set contains B-26 Marauder Bomber, F4U Corsair, and P-40 Flying Tiger.

1840 "ROAD MASTER" SET: (1970 – 1977)
Set contains auto transport with two cars, horse van with six horses, logger with three logs, and six other 4" toys.

1850 SUPER CONSTRUCTION SET: (1974 – 1978)
Set contains broad blade dozer, loader, roller, dump truck, cement truck, and four other 4" construction trucks.

1858 TOOTSIETOY MOTO-CROSS CYCLE SET: (1978 – 1979)
Set contains three die-cast metal frame motocross dirt bikes with rubber tires plus three flexible vinyl motocross drivers that attach to handlebars and footrests. Large die-cast metal wide body, sport truck and cycle trailer. Two large jump and hill climb track sections complete the set.

1860 SUPER SLICKS™ "6 PACK" SET: (1971 – 1974)
Set contains Panzer Wagon, Bandito, Desert Fox, Pie

Wagon, Twin Shaft, and the Dune Buster. Die-cast metal body is painted in show colors.

1862 TOOTSIETOY "CAREFREE DAYS" SET: (1979)
Set includes Blazer pickup truck with camper top, Blazer pickup with side boards, Blazer 4 x 4 pick-up, ATV vehicle, canoe trailer with two canoes, boat with die-cast metal trailer.

1865 TOOTSIETOY SUPER SPORT SET: (1977 – 1979)
Set contains two Scorpion helicopters, California van, large camper, two Honda motorcycles with trailer, Gremlin, speed boat and trailer, Jeepster, medium size motorcycle with trailer, Jeep, pickup truck, all-terrain vehicle, VW, Zodiac boat with trailer, and Bronco truck.

1870 TOOTSIETOY "BIG SPORT" SET: (1973 – 1976)
Set contains 19 different pieces. The speed boat, boat trailer, camper trailer, dirt bike, snowmobile with trailer, two Honda twin bikes with trailer, Attex, 3-wheeler, beach buggy, Jeepster, Bronco, Vega, Gremlin, Jeep, pickup, and VW bug.

1875 TOOTSIETOY EMERGENCY VEHICLE SET: (1977 – 1978)
Set contains 12 fire, police, and rescue vehicles, search light trailer, large helicopter, aerial ladder trucks, and eight various figures of rescue and fire personnel.

1872 TOOTSIETOY ROAD MASTER SET: (1978 – 1979)
Set consists of the following die-cast metal vehicles: tow truck, semi trailer rig, logger rig, auto transport with two cars, and eight other popular 4" cars and trucks.

2085 CAR CARRIER: (1970)
Set contains semi cab with car trailer, three Playmates vehicles with plastic removable drivers.

1985 CAR CARRIER: (1970)
Set contains semi cab with car trailer, three Playmates vehicles with plastic removable drivers.

2090 MOTHER GOOSE: (1970)
Hand-decorated Mother Goose nods her head when pulled. Peter's wife rides in a take-apart pumpkin. All the subjects are mounted on die-cast metal bases with sturdy hooks.

2405 MIDGET SPORT SETS: (1974 – 1979)
Set contains five different items in each set. Theme of sets range from car racing, recreation, and general sports.

2831 BLISTER CARDED "JAM PAC™": (1971 – 1979)
Set contains eight different cars and trucks packed under a clear, case style, blister.

2834 TOOTSIETOY "JAM PAC™ FLEET": (1970 – 1973)
Set contains eight die-cast metal cars and trucks and a set of three gas pumps on an island.

2835 TOOTSIETOY "JAM PAC™" SET: (1970 – 1971)
Set contains 10 top selling die-cast cars and trucks.

2850 JET FIGHTERS SET: (1970 – 1977)
Set contains three die-cast airplanes. Models of Swedish Saab J 35 "Dragon," U.S. Northrop F 5A "Little Tiger," West German McDonnel F4C "Phantom II," and French Dassault IIIC "Mirage."

2855 TRAIN SET: (1970 – 1971)
Set contains six-piece, highly detailed train. Cars include diesel engine, coal car, reefer, covered hopper, cattle car, and caboose.

2870 TOOTSIETOY CAR AND BOAT HITCH-UP® ASSORTMENT: (1978 – 1979)
Includes two different blister carded items. Each item has a die-cast metal car or truck with die-cast metal boat trailers and boats.

2871 TOOTSIE TOY CAR AND MOTORCYCLE HITCH-UP® ASSORTMENT: (1978 – 1979)
Includes two different blister carded items. Each item has a die-cast metal car or truck, die-cast metal cycle trailer, cycles with rubber tires and plated finishes.

2977 TOOTSIETOY JET FORMATION: (1979)
Set contains three all die-cast metal jet planes with steel axles and wheels. Each jet has a bright silver finish and colorful labels. Item length is 3".

5024 STROMBECKER "FAT KAT" HITCH-UPS: (1976 – 1978)
Assortment of two well-known Hitch Up combinations. High performance ski boat with boat trailer and "FAT KAT" pulling car. Motorcycle with sculptured trailer and "FAT KAT" pulling car.

5800 TOOTSIETOY BATTERY OPERATED ELECTRIC TRAIN: (1970 – 1971)
Set contains engine and three cars, 10 pieces of curved track, two sections straight track, and battery box with two forward speeds plus reverse, connecting wires and track cups.

SPECIAL ACKNOWLEDGMENTS

S. Butler Collection: Photographs of Florist, Market, Grocery, Federal vans, and post-war #1040 and #1041 fire trucks.

R. Smith Collection: Photograph of #720 Fly-n-Gyro airplane.

H. Stang Collection: For lending toys to be photographed. The GM series No-name coupe, 1935 Ford convertible coupe, #4666 silver racer, 1934 Ford wrecker, and #4700 Highway boxed set.

G. Willard Collection: Photographs taken by Evelyn Willard of her husband's toys. The Funnies Series six pieces, #190X four car transport, Lincoln wrecker, and Lincoln Zephyr.

S. Oznowich Collection: For lending toys to be photographed. The Farm boxed set, #5149 Highway set, Boeing 707 blister pack, Starbase Zeus boxed set, #198 Auto Transport, Contractor set, Graham convertible coupe with side spares, DC 4 Long Range Bomber plane, #1011 Tractor, Metro van with full decals. Anna Marie, his wife, for her #239 rare creme three-inch Woody wagon. Hunting up "O" gauge miniature people and landscape trees used in cover photograph.

Judith Andersen: Dodd Camera for excellent processing of all my film prints and helpful photo tips.

J. Shushok Collection: 1959 Chevrolet semi cab. (The Bus Stop)

ABOUT THE AUTHOR

I always enjoyed my Tootsietoys as a small child. I joined the United States Army in 1962, and served my country in Germany for three years. Returning home in 1965, I happened to discover one small Tootsietoy CJ3 Army Jeep in an old desk drawer. This, I later found out, was the sole survivor from my childhood. I wanted to gather more toys and start a collection of America's first die-cast toys.

I started attending antique shows and the larger toy shows to search out and purchase more Tootsietoys to build a nice collection. The only regret I have is not buying the pre-war toys first. But making only $2.36 an hour at a power plant in 1965 did limit my buying power somewhat. Along with rent, utilities, and insurances, I did however still manage to buy a few toys when I could spare the extra cash.

Thirty years later at age 51, I still enjoy this rewarding popular hobby of collecting Tootsietoys and learning new information about them every day. I am still searching for the small handful of items I lack for a complete collection of Tootsietoys.

All the toys and boxed sets pictured in my new second edition book are from my own personal collection, with the exception of the few photographs supplied by fellow collectors or toys lent to me to photograph for this book.

Happy Collecting!

David E. Richter

◆ BOOKS ON GLASS AND POTTERY ◆

This is only a partial listing of the books on antiques that are available from Collector Books. All books are well illustrated and contain current values. Most of the following books are available from your local bookseller, antique dealer, or public library. If you are unable to locate certain titles in your area, you may order by mail from COLLECTOR BOOKS, P.O. Box 3009, Paducah, KY 42002-3009. Customers with Visa or MasterCard may phone in orders from 7:00–4:00 CST, Monday–Friday, Toll Free 1-800-626-5420. Add $2.00 for postage for the first book ordered and $0.30 for each additional book. Include item number, title, and price when ordering. Allow 14 to 21 days for delivery.

GLASSWARE

1006	**Cambridge Glass** Reprint 1930–1934	$14.95
1007	**Cambridge Glass** Reprint 1949–1953	$14.95
2310	**Children's Glass Dishes, China & Furniture**, Vol. I, Lechler	$19.95
1627	**Children's Glass Dishes, China & Furniture**, Vol. II, Lechler	$19.95
3719	Coll. **Glassware from the 40's, 50's & 60's**, 2nd Ed., Florence	$19.95
2352	Collector's Encyclopedia of **Akro Agate Glassware**, Florence	$14.95
1810	Collector's Encyclopedia of **American Art Glass**, Shuman	$29.95
3312	Collector's Encyclopedia of **Children's Dishes**, Whitmyer	$19.95
3724	Collector's Encyclopedia of **Depression Glass**, 11th Ed., Florence	$19.95
1664	Collector's Encyclopedia of **Heisey Glass**, 1925–1938, Bredehoft	$24.95
3905	Collector's Encyclopedia of **Milk Glass**, Newbound	$24.95
1523	Colors In **Cambridge Glass**, National Cambridge Soceity	$19.95
1843	Covered **Animal Dishes**, Grist	$14.95
2275	**Czechoslovakian Glass** and Collectibles, Barta	$16.95
3882	**Elegant Glassware** of the Depression Era, 6th Ed., Florence	$19.95
1380	Encylopedia of **Pattern Glass**, McClain	$12.95
3981	Ever's Standard **Cut Glass** Value Guide	$12.95
3725	**Fostoria**, Pressed, Blown & Hand Molded Shapes, Kerr	$24.95
3883	**Fostoria Stemware**, The Crystal for America, Long & Seate	$24.95
3318	**Glass Animals** of the Depression Era, Garmon & Spencer	$19.95
1008	**Imperial Glass** Reprint 1904–1938, Archer	$14.95
3886	**Kitchen Glassware** of the Depression Years, 5th Ed., Florence	$19.95
2394	**Oil Lamps II**, Glass Kerosene Lamps	$24.95
3889	Pocket Guide to **Depression Glass**, 9th Ed., Florence	$9.95
3739	Standard Encylopedia of **Carnival Glass**, 4th Ed., Edwards	$24.95
3740	Standard **Carnival Glass** Price Guide, 9th Ed.	$9.95
3974	Standard Encylopedia of **Opalescent Glass**, Edwards	$19.95
1848	**Very Rare Glassware** of the Depression Years, Florence	$24.95
2140	**Very Rare Glassware** of the Depression Years, 2nd Series, Florence	$24.95
3326	**Very Rare Glassware** of the Depression Years, 3rd Series, Florence	$24.95
3909	**Very Rare Glassware** of the Depression Years, 4th Series, Florence	$24.95
2224	World of **Salt Shakers**, 2nd Ed., Lechner	$24.95

POTTERY

1312	**Blue & White Stoneware**, McNerney	$9.95
1958	So. Potteries **Blue Ridge Dinnerware**, 3rd Ed., Newbound	$14.95
1959	**Blue Willow**, 2nd Ed., Gaston	$14.95
3816	Collectible **Vernon Kilns**, Nelson	$24.95
3311	Collecting **Yellow Ware** – Id. & Value Guide, McAllister	$16.95
1373	Collector's Encyclopedia of **American Dinnerware**, Cunningham	$24.95
3815	Collector's Encyclopedia of **Blue Ridge Dinnerware**, Newbound	$19.95
2272	Collector's Encyclopedia of **California Pottery**, Chipman	$24.95
3811	Collector's Encyclopedia of **Colorado Pottery**, Carlton	$24.95
2133	Collector's Encyclopedia of **Cookie Jars**, Roerig	$24.95
3723	Collector's Encyclopedia of **Cookie Jars**, Volume II, Roerig	$24.95
3429	Collector's Encyclopedia of **Cowan Pottery**, Saloff	$24.95
2209	Collector's Encyclopedia of **Fiesta**, 7th Ed., Huxford	$19.95
3961	Collector's Encyclopedia of **Early Noritake**, Alden	$24.95
1439	Collector's Encyclopedia of **Flow Blue China**, Gaston	$19.95
3812	Collector's Encyclopedia of **Flow Blue China**, 2nd Ed., Gaston	$24.95

1813	Collector's Encyclopedia of **Geisha Girl Porcelain**, Litts	$19.95
3813	Collector's Encyclopedia of **Hall China**, 2nd Ed., Whitmyer	$24.95
3431	Collector's Encyclopedia of **Homer Laughlin China**, Jasper	$24.95
1276	Collector's Encyclopedia of **Hull Pottery**, Roberts	$19.95
3962	Collector's Encyclopedia of **Lefton China**, DeLozier	$19.95
2210	Collector's Encyclopedia of **Limoges Porcelain**, 2nd Ed., Gaston	$24.95
2334	Collector's Encyclopedia of **Majolica Pottery**, Katz-Marks	$19.95
1358	Collector's Encyclopedia of **McCoy Pottery**, Huxford	$19.95
3963	Collector's Encyclopedia of Metlox Potteries, Gibbs Jr.	$24.95
3313	Collector's Encyclopedia of **Niloak**, Gifford	$19.95
3837	Collector's Encyclopedia of **Nippon Porcelain I**, Van Patten	$24.95
2089	Collector's Ency. of **Nippon Porcelain**, 2nd Series, Van Patten	$24.95
1665	Collector's Ency. of **Nippon Porcelain**, 3rd Series, Van Patten	$24.95
3836	**Nippon Porcelain** Price Guide, Van Patten	$9.95
1447	Collector's Encyclopedia of **Noritake**, Van Patten	$19.95
3432	Collector's Encyclopedia of **Noritake**, 2nd Series, Van Patten	$24.95
1037	Collector's Encyclopedia of **Occupied Japan**, Vol. I, Florence	$14.95
1038	Collector's Encyclopedia of **Occupied Japan**, Vol. II, Florence	$14.95
2088	Collector's Encyclopedia of **Occupied Japan**, Vol. III, Florence	$14.95
2019	Collector's Encyclopedia of **Occupied Japan**, Vol. IV, Florence	$14.95
2335	Collector's Encyclopedia of **Occupied Japan**, Vol. V, Florence	$14.95
3964	Collector's Encyclopedia of **Pickard China**, Reed	$24.95
1311	Collector's Encyclopedia of **R.S. Prussia**, 1st Series, Gaston	$24.95
1715	Collector's Encyclopedia of **R.S. Prussia**, 2nd Series, Gaston	$24.95
3726	Collector's Encyclopedia of **R.S. Prussia**, 3rd Series, Gaston	$24.95
3877	Collector's Encyclopedia of **R.S. Prussia**, 4th Series, Gaston	$24.95
1034	Collector's Encyclopedia of **Roseville Pottery**, Huxford	$19.95
1035	Collector's Encyclopedia of **Roseville Pottery**, 2nd Ed., Huxford	$19.95
3357	**Roseville** Price Guide No. 10	$9.95
2083	Collector's Encyclopedia of **Russel Wright** Designs, Kerr	$19.95
3965	Collector's Encyclopedia of **Sasha Brastoff**, Conti, Bethany & Seay	$24.95
3314	Collector's Encyclopedia of **Van Briggle** Art Pottery, Sasicki	$24.95
2111	Collector's Encyclopedia of **Weller Pottery**, Huxford	$29.95
3452	Coll. Guide to Country Stoneware & Pottery, Raycraft	$11.95
2077	Coll. Guide to **Country Stoneware & Pottery**, 2nd Series, Raycraft	$14.95
3433	Collector's Guide To **Harker Pottery** - U.S.A., Colbert	$17.95
3434	Coll. Guide to **Hull Pottery**, The Dinnerware Line, Gick-Burke	$16.95
3876	Collector's Guide to **Lu-Ray Pastels**, Meehan	$18.95
2339	Collector's Guide to **Shawnee Pottery**, Vanderbilt	$19.95
1425	**Cookie Jars**, Westfall	$9.95
3440	**Cookie Jars**, Book II, Westfall	$19.95
3435	Debolt's Dictionary of **American Pottery Marks**	$17.95
2076	Early **Roseville Pottery**, Huxford	$7.95
1917	**Head Vases**, Identification & Values, Cole	$14.95
2379	Lehner's Ency. of **U.S. Marks** on Pottery, Porcelain & China	$24.95
3825	**Puritan Pottery**, Morris	$24.95
1670	**Red Wing Collectibles**, DePasquale	$9.95
1440	**Red Wing Stoneware**, DePasquale	$9.95
2350	**Royal Copley**, Wolfe	$14.95
2351	More **Royal Copley**, Wolfe	$14.95
3738	**Shawnee Pottery**, Mangus	$24.95
3327	**Watt Pottery** – Identification & Value Guide, Morris	$19.95

BOOKS ON COLLECTIBLES

This is only a partial listing of the books on antiques that are available from Collector Books. All books are well illustrated and contain current values. Most of the following books are available from your local bookseller, antique dealer, or public library. If you are unable to locate certain titles in your area, you may order by mail from COLLECTOR BOOKS, P.O. Box 3009, Paducah, KY 42002-3009. Customers with Visa or MasterCard may phone in orders from 7:00–4:00 CST, Monday–Friday, Toll Free 1-800-626-5420. Add $2.00 for postage for the first book ordered and $0.30 for each additional book. Include item number, title, and price when ordering. Allow 14 to 21 days for delivery.

DOLLS, FIGURES & TEDDY BEARS

2382	**Advertising Dolls**, Identification & Values, Robison & Sellers	$9.95
2079	**Barbie** Doll Fashions, Volume I, Eames	$24.95
3957	**Barbie** Exclusives, Rana	$18.95
3310	**Black Dolls**, 1820–1991, Perkins	$17.95
3873	**Black Dolls**, Book II, Perkins	$17.95
3810	**Chatty Cathy** Dolls, Lewis	$15.95
2021	Collector's **Male Action Figures**, Manos	$14.95
1529	Collector's Encyclopedia of **Barbie** Dolls, DeWein	$19.95
3727	Collector's Guide to **Ideal Dolls**, Izen	$18.95
3728	Collector's Guide to Miniature **Teddy Bears**, Powell	$17.95
4506	**Dolls in Uniform**, Bourgeois	$18.95
3967	Collector's Guide to **Trolls**, Peterson	$19.95
1067	**Madame Alexander** Dolls, Smith	$19.95
3971	**Madame Alexander** Dolls Price Guide #20, Smith	$9.95
2185	**Modern Collector's Dolls** I, Smith	$17.95
2186	**Modern Collector's Dolls** II, Smith	$17.95
2187	**Modern Collector's Dolls** III, Smith	$17.95
2188	**Modern Collector's Dolls** IV, Smith	$17.95
2189	**Modern Collector's Dolls** V, Smith	$17.95
3733	**Modern Collector's Dolls**, Sixth Series, Smith	$24.95
3991	**Modern Collector's Dolls**, Seventh Series, Smith	$24.95
3472	**Modern Collector's Dolls** Update, Smith	$9.95
3972	Patricia Smith's **Doll Values**, Antique to Modern, 11th Edition	$12.95
3826	Story of **Barbie**, Westenhouser	$19.95
1513	**Teddy Bears & Steiff** Animals, Mandel	$9.95
1817	**Teddy Bears & Steiff** Animals, 2nd Series, Mandel	$19.95
2084	**Teddy Bears, Annalee's & Steiff** Animals, 3rd Series, Mandel	$19.95
1808	Wonder of **Barbie**, Manos	$9.95
1430	World of **Barbie** Dolls, Manos	$9.95

TOYS, MARBLES & CHRISTMAS COLLECTIBLES

3427	**Advertising Character** Collectibles, Dotz	$17.95
2333	Antique & Collector's **Marbles**, 3rd Ed., Grist	$9.95
3827	Antique & Collector's **Toys**, 1870–1950, Longest	$24.95
3956	Baby Boomer **Games**, Identification & Value Guide, Polizzi	$24.95
1514	Character **Toys** & Collectibles, Longest	$19.95
1750	Character **Toys** & Collector's, 2nd Series, Longest	$19.95
3717	**Christmas** Collectibles, 2nd Edition, Whitmyer	$24.95
1752	**Christmas** Ornaments, Lights & Decorations, Johnson	$19.95
3874	Collectible Coca-Cola Toy **Trucks**, deCourtivron	$24.95
2338	Collector's Encyclopedia of **Disneyana**, Longest, Stern	$24.95
2151	Collector's Guide to **Tootsietoys**, Richter	$16.95
3436	Grist's Big Book of **Marbles**	$19.95
3970	Grist's Machine-Made & Contemporary **Marbles**, 2nd Ed.	$9.95
3732	**Matchbox®** Toys, 1948 to 1993, Johnson	$18.95
3823	**Mego** Toys, An Illustrated Value Guide, Chrouch	15.95
1540	**Modern Toys** 1930–1980, Baker	$19.95
3888	**Motorcycle** Toys, Antique & Contemporary, Gentry/Downs	$18.95
3891	Schroeder's Collectible **Toys**, Antique to Modern Price Guide	$17.95
1886	Stern's Guide to **Disney** Collectibles	$14.95
2139	Stern's Guide to **Disney** Collectibles, 2nd Series	$14.95
3975	Stern's Guide to **Disney** Collectibles, 3rd Series	$18.95
2028	**Toys**, Antique & Collectible, Longest	$14.95
3975	**Zany Characters** of the Ad World, Lamphier	$16.95

JEWELRY, HATPINS, WATCHES & PURSES

1712	Antique & Collector's **Thimbles** & Accessories, Mathis	$19.95
1748	Antique **Purses**, Revised Second Ed., Holiner	$19.95
1278	Art Nouveau & Art Deco **Jewelry**, Baker	$9.95
3875	Collecting Antique **Stickpins**, Kerins	$16.95
3722	Collector's Ency. of **Compacts, Carryalls & Face Powder Boxes**, Mueller	$24.95
3992	Complete Price Guide to **Watches**, #15, Shugart	$21.95
1716	Fifty Years of Collector's **Fashion Jewelry**, 1925-1975, Baker	$19.95
1424	**Hatpins** & Hatpin Holders, Baker	$9.95
1181	100 Years of Collectible **Jewelry**, Baker	$9.95
2348	20th Century Fashionable Plastic **Jewelry**, Baker	$19.95
3830	Vintage **Vanity Bags & Purses**, Gerson	$24.95

FURNITURE

1457	American **Oak** Furniture, McNerney	$9.95
3716	American **Oak** Furniture, Book II, McNerney	$12.95
1118	Antique **Oak** Furniture, Hill	$7.95
2132	Collector's Encyclopedia of **American** Furniture, Vol. I, Swedberg	$24.95
2271	Collector's Encyclopedia of **American** Furniture, Vol. II, Swedberg	$24.95
3720	Collector's Encyclopedia of **American** Furniture, Vol. III, Swedberg	$24.95
1437	Collector's Guide to **Country** Furniture, Raycraft	$9.95
3878	Collector's Guide to **Oak** Furniture, George	$12.95
1755	**Furniture** of the **Depression Era**, Swedberg	$19.95
3906	**Heywood-Wakefield** Modern Furniture, Rouland	$18.95
1965	**Pine** Furniture, Our American Heritage, McNerney	$14.95
1885	**Victorian** Furniture, Our American Heritage, McNerney	$9.95
3829	**Victorian** Furniture, Our American Heritage, Book II, McNerney	$9.95
3869	**Victorian** Furniture books, 2 volume set, McNerney	$19.90

INDIANS, GUNS, KNIVES, TOOLS, PRIMITIVES

1868	Antique **Tools**, Our American Heritage, McNerney	$9.95
2015	Archaic **Indian** Points & Knives, Edler	$14.95
1426	**Arrowheads** & Projectile Points, Hothem	$7.95
1668	**Flint Blades** & Projectile Points of the North American Indian, Tully	$24.95
2279	**Indian** Artifacts of the Midwest, Hothem	$14.95
3885	**Indian** Artifacts of the Midwest, Book II, Hothem	$16.95
1964	**Indian** Axes & Related Stone Artifacts, Hothem	$14.95
2023	**Keen Kutter** Collectibles, Heuring	$14.95
3887	**Modern Guns**, Identification & Values, 10th Ed., Quertermous	$12.95
2164	**Primitives**, Our American Heritage, McNerney	$9.95
1759	**Primitives**, Our American Heritage, Series II, McNerney	$14.95
3325	Standard **Knife** Collector's Guide, 2nd Ed., Ritchie & Stewart	$12.95 .

PAPER COLLECTIBLES & BOOKS

1441	Collector's Guide to **Post Cards**, Wood	$9.95
2081	Guide to Collecting **Cookbooks**, Allen	$14.95
3969	Huxford's **Old Book** Value Guide, 7th Ed.	$19.95
3821	Huxford's **Paperback** Value Guide	$19.95
2080	Price Guide to **Cookbooks** & Recipe Leaflets, Dickinson	$9.95
2346	**Sheet Music** Reference & Price Guide, Pafik & Guiheen	$18.95

OTHER COLLECTIBLES

2280	Advertising **Playing Cards**, Grist	$16.95
2269	Antique **Brass & Copper** Collectibles, Gaston	$16.95
1880	Antique **Iron**, McNerney	$9.95
3872	Antique **Tins**, Dodge	$24.95
1714	**Black** Collectibles, Gibbs	$19.95
1128	**Bottle** Pricing Guide, 3rd Ed., Cleveland	$7.95
3959	**Cereal Box** Bonanza, The 1950's, Bruce	$19.95
3718	Collector's **Aluminum**, Grist	$16.95
3445	Collectible **Cats**, An Identification & Value Guide, Fyke	$18.95
1634	Collector's Ency. of Figural & Novelty **Salt & Pepper Shakers**, Davern	$19.95
2020	Collector's Ency. of Figural & Novelty **Salt & Pepper Shakers**, Vol. II, Davern	$19.95
2018	Collector's Encyclopedia of **Granite Ware**, Greguire	$24.95
3430	Collector's Encyclopedia of **Granite Ware**, Book II, Greguire	$24.95
3879	Collector's Guide to Antique **Radios**, 3rd Ed., Bunis	$18.95
1916	Collector's Guide to **Art Deco**, Gaston	$14.95
3880	Collector's Guide to **Cigarette Lighters**, Flanagan	$17.95
1537	Collector's Guide to **Country Baskets**, Raycraft	$9.95
3966	Collector's Guide to **Inkwells**, Identification & Values, Badders	$18.95
3881	Collector's Guide to **Novelty Radios**, Bunis/Breed	$18.95
3729	Collector's Guide to **Snow Domes**, Guarnaccia	$18.95
3730	Collector's Guide to **Transistor Radios**, Bunis	$15.95
2276	**Decoys**, Kangas	$24.95
1629	**Doorstops**, Identification & Values, Bertoia	$9.95
3968	**Fishing Lure** Collectibles, Murphy/Edmisten	$24.95
3817	**Flea Market Trader**, 9th Ed., Huxford	$12.95
3819	**General Store** Collectibles, Wilson	$24.95
2215	Goldstein's **Coca-Cola** Collectibles	$16.95
3884	Huxford's Collector's **Advertising**, 2nd Ed.	$24.95
2216	**Kitchen Antiques**, 1790–1940, McNerney	$14.95
1782	1,000 **Fruit Jars**, 5th Edition, Schroeder	$5.95
3321	Ornamental & Figural **Nutcrackers**, Rittenhouse	$16.95
2026	**Railroad** Collectibles, 4th Ed., Baker	$14.95
1632	**Salt & Pepper Shakers**, Guarnaccia	$9.95
1888	**Salt & Pepper Shakers** II, Identification & Value Guide, Book II, Guarnaccia	$14.95
2220	**Salt & Pepper Shakers** III, Guarnaccia	$14.95
3443	**Salt & Pepper Shakers** IV, Guarnaccia	$18.95
2096	**Silverplated Flatware**, Revised 4th Edition, Hagan	$14.95
1922	Standard **Old Bottle** Price Guide, Sellari	$14.95
3892	**Toy & Miniature Sewing Machines**, Thomas	$18.95
3828	Value Guide to **Advertising Memorabilia**, Summers	$18.95
3977	Value Guide to **Gas Station** Memorabilia	$24.95
3444	**Wanted to Buy**, 5th Edition	$9.95

Schroeder's ANTIQUES Price Guide

. . . is the #1 best-selling antiques & collectibles value guide on the market today, and here's why . . .

Schroeder's ANTIQUES Price Guide

OUR #1 BEST SELLER!

Identification & Values Of Over 50,000 Antiques & Collectibles

8½ x 11, 608 Pages, $14.95

• *More than 300 advisors, well-known dealers, and top-notch collectors work together with our editors to bring you accurate information regarding pricing and identification.*

• *More than 45,000 items in almost 500 categories are listed along with hundreds of sharp original photos that illustrate not only the rare and unusual, but the common, popular collectibles as well.*

• *Each large close-up shot shows important details clearly. Every subject is represented with histories and background information, a feature not found in any of our competitors' publications.*

• *Our editors keep abreast of newly developing trends, often adding several new categories a year as the need arises.*

If it merits the interest of today's collector, you'll find it in *Schroeder's*. And you can feel confident that the information we publish is up to date and accurate. Our advisors thoroughly check each category to spot inconsistencies, listings that may not be entirely reflective of market dealings, and lines too vague to be of merit. Only the best of the lot remains for publication.

Without doubt, you'll find
SCHROEDER'S ANTIQUES PRICE GUIDE
the only one to buy for
reliable information and values.

COLLECTOR BOOKS
A Division of Schroeder Publishing Co., Inc.